Rockhounding
Wyoming

by
Kenneth Lee Graham

Consulting Editor
W.R.C. Shedenhelm
former Senior Editor of *Rock & Gem Magazine*

FALCON

Falcon Press® Publishing Co., Inc.
Helena, Montana

A FALCON GUIDE

Falcon Press is continually expanding its list of recreational guide-books. All books include detailed descriptions, accurate maps, and all the information necessary for enjoyable trips. You can order extra copies of this book and get information and prices for other Falcon guidebooks by writing Falcon Press, P.O. Box 1718, Helena, MT 59624 or calling toll free 1-800-582-2665. Also, please ask for a free copy of our current catalog. Our e-mail address is: falconbk@ix.netcom.com

Printed in the United States of America.

All black-and-white photos by Kenneth Lee Graham.
Cover photo by Kenneth Lee Graham.

Library of Congress Cataloging-in-Publication Data

Rockhounding Wyoming / by Kennerth Lee Graham
    p.   cm.
"A Falcon Guide"—T.p. verso
Includes index.
ISBN 1-56044-445-2 (pbk.)
1. Rocks—Wyoming—Collection and preservation—Guidebooks
2. Minerals—Wyoming—Collection and preservation—Guidebooks
3. Wyoming—Guidebooks. I. Title
QE445.W8G7   1996
552.09787—dc20   96-22101
                                                             CIP

CAUTION

Outdoor recreation activities are by their very nature potentially hazard-ous. All participants in such activities must assume the responsibility for their own actions and safety. The information contained in this guidebook cannot replace sound judgment and good decision-making skills, which help reduce the risk exposure, nor does the scope of this book allow for disclo-sure of all the potential hazards and risks involved in such activities.

Learn as much as possible about the outdoor recreation activities in which you participate, prepare for the unexpected, and be cautious. The reward will be a safer and more enjoyable experience.

   Text pages printed on recycled paper.

"It seems that the strangeness and wonder are emphasized here in the desert . . . . The extreme clarity of the desert light is equaled by the extreme individualism of desert life forms."

—Edward Abbey

CONTENTS

ACKNOWLEDGMENTS

Many days of discovery from childhood to the present have been preceded by private counsel. Some advisors were rockhounds with questions of their own, others were local residents joyfully sharing information on some of the otherwise unknown qualities of their homeland. My quest could never have been as successful without this shared knowledge.

My special thanks go to all, though I have no way of recalling the multitude of names of the folks I visited briefly at gas stations, rock shops, or restaurants.

Thanks especially go to Brent Bestrum, geologist, for the time spent unveiling the mysteries of my areas of interest. Gretchen Hurley, geologist, also played a vital part in the hunt. These two are not the only sources, but their patient explanations made geology understandable for me.

There are more words that can be said than should fill this brief space. However the help I credit to some sources does not mean to imply that others would not help. It just means we never connected.

I want to thank Judd McDonald of Lander, Willie and Lorrie Adams of Casper, and Richard Green of Shoshone, Dave and Carol Bernhardt of Billings, and Ray Harris of the Wyoming State Geological Survey. Last but not least, I want to express my gratitude to my wife and son, Sandy and Derrick, for their enthusiastic support and patience. At the risk of forgetting others, I am bringing this list to a close. The forgetfulness does not make the information less valuable, it only hints of my old age.

WYOMING ROCKHOUNDING SITES

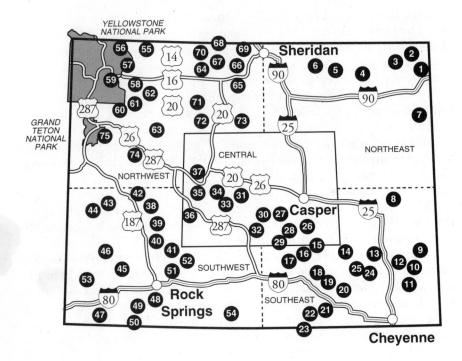

MAP LEGEND

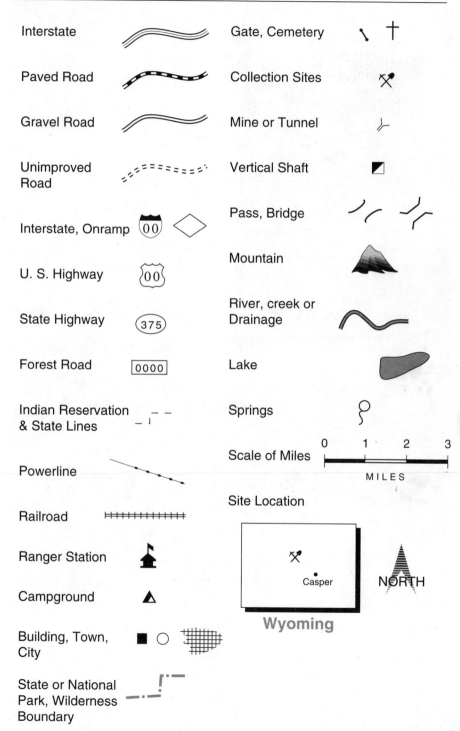

Interstate	Gate, Cemetery
Paved Road	Collection Sites
Gravel Road	Mine or Tunnel
Unimproved Road	Vertical Shaft
Interstate, Onramp 00	Pass, Bridge
U. S. Highway 00	Mountain
State Highway 375	River, creek or Drainage
Forest Road 0000	Lake
Indian Reservation & State Lines	Springs
Powerline	Scale of Miles
Railroad	Site Location
Ranger Station	
Campground	
Building, Town, City	
State or National Park, Wilderness Boundary	

Scale of Miles
0 1 2 3
MILES

Site Location

Casper

Wyoming

NORTH

Banded agate from the Mineral Hills site can be large enough to slab.

ABOUT THIS BOOK

My interest in rocks first began when I saw my uncle's living room display. The individual beauty of each specimen captured my interest and launched me on my own quest for similar treasures. With unquenchable thirst I drank in detailed directions to selected sites—but I found that several hours of attentive listening were not enough time to absorb all his wisdom. Many phone calls and quick visits added to my ever increasing knowledge and I soon discovered other people with the same burning interest. My knowledge not only increased, but I became a source of information as well.

Many benefits came with my quest. Each treasure displayed carries an associated memory, like a breathtaking landscape, or a spine-chilling encounter with a grizzly bear, a rattlesnake, or other wild animal. With these pleasures came a fellowship with others who shared my passion for rockhounding

Among other lessons of life, I found that not all people are interested in looking for rocks. The beauty is generally acknowledged, but love of hunting and displaying the stones seems to fall randomly among many types of people. This book is not meant to be a complete guide, nor a scientific explanation of rocks. It is simply an introduction to a fascinating treasure hunt for those who would dare to follow.

Rockhounding is changing. Within our current political structure, many sites are presently closed and more closures are planned. Increasing interest and public involvement in land management decisions may help keep public lands open to rockhounding. But in spite of these changes, nothing can compare to the thrill of hearing a first-time finder exclaim, "Wow, look at this!"

I am sure there are greedy rockhounds out there, but in my experience, the majority desire to share their discoveries. Please accept this enticement to begin adding to your own treasure map, not just for yourself, but for those who will follow you.

This book is intended to be a self-study course on geological deposits, without all the hard-to-pronounce words. I hope the reader will observe the landscape, and with discernment make new discoveries.

Sometimes the joy is in the search itself.

INTRODUCTION

Wyoming means "high prairie," a derivative of an Indian word *mecheweaming*, which originally was understood to mean "at the big flat." Over time, this meaning has been redefined to "high prairie," which in Wyoming has a broad interpretation because some areas look more like a desert.

I have been told that Wyoming's red desert is the largest unfenced area in the lower forty-eight states. When gazing over the expanse from any one of several overviews that is easy to believe. Most of Wyoming is public land, a wide open expanse decorated with high mountain majesty.

Central Wyoming holds the most interest for rockhounds with jade as the drawing-card. Though the apple green variety is rare, there are still very fine pieces being found. It is also the home of fluorescent Sweetwater agate and other prized specimens.

Southeastern Wyoming offers some extensive options including diamond-bearing kimberlite. The land containing these beauties is all carefully regulated, however. Other rarities include Guernsey agate, bloodstone, fossils, petrified wood, onyx, and agate. Some metals are found in the higher mountains though it is hard to look for specimens in the distracting beauty of the high country, especially after the drive through so much nothingness. There are fewer mines to search through, with a combination of reclamation and private enterprise depleting their numbers. Some creative mine owners have developed old mining claims into residential sites in very remote parts of the country.

Northeastern Wyoming does not have the variety found to the south but offers some interesting if not unique minerals. Fluorite is found in the Bear Lodge mountains, along with agate and fossils. Much of this land is privately owned, making rockhounding a little more complicated. But with the right approach and patience access may be granted, providing excellent opportunities for the persistent.

Southwestern Wyoming is probably best known for fossils. The fossil fish is the most well known, but certainly not the only attraction. "Fossil" agates and the highly prized opalized wood from Eden valley draw many a seeker.

Northwestern Wyoming offers Wind River Iris or rainbow agate, named for the way it diffuses sunlight when thinly sliced. Spanish Point agates are also a precious attraction, though the biggest drawing factor is a trip through Yellowstone National Park. This wonderland is discussed in its own chapter and though the specimens in this spectacular park are not to be removed, a trip is absolutely in order.

Wildlife

Rattlesnakes top the danger list for me, though bears are probably more deadly. For the most part, the snakes I have encountered were more afraid of me than I was of them. Be mindful of the direction they go and don't follow.

Large game is a welcome attraction when treated with common sense and

This fellow is defiantly defending his right to this sun warmed asphalt on a cool evening.

respect. Antelope seem to dominate otherwise desolate expanses of sage brush and can provide some interesting viewing. Antelope prefer to go under, rather than over, fences, and their antics provide an interesting side show at times.

Deer are common along roads around sunrise and sunset. A watchful eye is necessary to avoid a collision that can kill the deer and put an abrupt end to a rockhounding trip. They are hardest to see in the early morning or late evening.

Elk, buffalo, and moose are seen most frequently in Yellowstone Park, though this is not the only place to view their majesty. Bears are not as common a sight as in the past. At one point in my childhood I remember parking in line with countless other cars blocking the roadway in Yellowstone Park. At first we were entertained by the four or five bears sitting in various spots. Our interest soon turned to great concern as not one but several people got out of their vehicles and risked life and limb to hand-feed the furry beggars. As a result the Park Service has moved the bears away from the roads. They are around, however, and can pose a serious threat in the backcountry. Any visitor to bear country should check with park personnel for trouble spots and current information on safe hiking and camping.

While large animals may be more dangerous, the most irritating critter to me is the pesky mosquito. There are ticks, too, but they do not buzz in my ear at night and keep me awake. Bug repellent is of great value, but it is often expensive or unavailable in remote areas, so bring what you need with you.

Antelope provide a pleasant seek-and-find exercise during long prairie drives.

There are a lot of miles between places in Wyoming, so a word to the wise should be sufficient.

Rock Shops

Rock shops come and go. A sizable shop existed in Lusk but is no longer there. Other unadvertised or unknown shops are likely out there that have eluded me.

Some of the shops listed are for sale with an uncertain future. Others keep non-traditional hours. So, like the treasures sought in the vast Wyoming terrain, connecting with the local rock shop may require a certain amount of effort. The information gained from these local enthusiasts makes finding them well worth the time spent.

With that in mind, the best that can be said for the list of shops in Appendix B is that it represents a starting point.

Wyoming Weather

Wyoming's high elevation creates a relatively cool climate. A hot sunny day will often require a coat at day's end. This is especially true of the high country surrounding the vast desert basins between mountain ranges. Average rainfall is only 14.5 inches per year, though it is obviously not evenly

Not all that looks dry is. We broke through here on a July trip a full day after the rain.

distributed. The eastern portion of the state seems to get the greater share of moisture while the southwestern parts look quite forsaken. When the drier portions do get moisture, dirt roads go through some dramatic changes.

Wyoming wind will leave a permanent impression on all first-time visitors. A story once circulated through a mining camp in central Wyoming about a local wind indicator. Supposedly a half-inch log chain was left dangling just off the ground on a pole near a public gathering place. If the chain held steady at 45 degrees from the vertical pole it was an ordinary day. A truly windy day was when this chain stretched out horizontal. There have been days when it would be easy to believe this story.

Storms can be fast and furious in any part of Wyoming, though they seem to be much more aggressive in the wide open desert. The wind makes things much more complicated, and if your travels take you into some distant backcountry it might be best to set and wait. Though it is unlikely that many people will be exploring during the winter months, it should be noted that the gates on the highways are not for livestock. When those gates block the road, it is closed to vehicular traffic or to public travel.

For the most part the weather in summer will provide plenty of quality conditions for the persistent. Early morning is generally the quietest time with winds increasing by early afternoon.

Finding Your Way

I have made every effort to provide accurate maps and mileage counts. The major problem of course is that odometer readings vary. Therefore, take the mileage reported as approximate.

Destinations often are visible long before you get there. It is such a wide open country that landmarks appearing close are really some distance away. But don't be afraid to stop and check out areas on the way. Unforeseen treasures and beauty may be discovered.

Mountain Safety—Driving

Many, if not all, of the mountain roads and jeep trails will be one lane with very few places wide enough for two vehicles to pass. Although Wyoming does not boast a very large population, there will still be times when you will meet another vehicle. It is important to be prepared to avoid making a complicated procedure more hazardous.

The most important rule is to not panic. Many accidents and injuries can be avoided with a little thinking time. A hurried decision can overlook minor details that turn into major trouble. Another important rule to be aware of is that the vehicle traveling uphill has the right of way. The reason for this is that it is much more dangerous to try to back down a hill than up one. This is hard to understand sometimes, but it is easy for a vehicle backing down to get out of control.

Try to remember where the wider places are. It will help your peace of mind if you have to back up to one. Keep an eye out for approaching vehicles as far ahead as possible. Even though you may be going uphill, if you see a vehicle coming and you can pull over near where you are, you may prevent a confrontation. Unfortunately, not all drivers use this courtesy and will just keep coming as though the road will suddenly widen out. Don't try to pass the other vehicle or let it pass you, unless you are 100 percent certain that it is safe to do so. If you have to back down any hill, for any reason, do it slowly.

You may encounter horses on mountain roads more often than vehicles. Most of the mountain roads are in fact entry points to wilderness areas where motorized vehicles are not allowed past designated points. When meeting horseback riders it is a matter of country courtesy to pull off as far as possible or get out of the way at the nearest point and shut off your vehicle. Not all of the horses being ridden are acquainted with motor noise. Not too mention the possibility that the rider may be inexperienced as well.

Many of the areas described in this guide are a long way from service stations. Keep your fuel tank full, carry extra water, and make sure your spare tire is properly inflated and that you have adequate tools and equipment to change a tire. Tire chains, a shovel, and a tow chain or rope also may come in handy.

Also, be wary of old tracks and ruts that may look like a road. Remnants of century-old trails such as the great western movement along the Oregon Trail and old stage coach routes still are visible in parts of Wyoming. The vehicle that made those tracks could very well have been a covered wagon. If you are not sure of the road conditions ahead, don't go.

Abandoned Mine Safety

For a rockhound many of the treasures awaiting discovery are found in the waste piles at mines. Any other goodies left underground are not worth the risk, under any circumstance. Even in the productive life of an active mine, death shows no mercy. More than one funeral is buried in my memory as a reminder of the danger deceptively hidden in countless ways, both above and below the surface. If trained, experienced miners are subject to death and injury in a working mine, how can an inexperienced person expect to safely enter and explore old, unmaintained mine workings? Don't do it!

Any hole even if it looks shallow is not even remotely safe. In the past, deep shafts were bulkheaded with timbers about 12 feet below the surface. The sides of the shaft would then be blasted to cover the bulkhead with rock. This was done to keep enterprising thieves from entering and "high grading" ore. Time and decay are continually weakening those bulkhead timbers, often with no visible sign of change.

Air quality is another concern. I have worked in a large and deep gold mine where two miners suffocated after taking a "mine tour" in some abandoned workings. Among other qualities, the air in a mine itself can be filled with poison such as the radon gasses generated in uranium mines. Just because there is a breeze fluffing the hair on your forehead doesn't mean it's healthy.

Children demand the most attention and must be watched constantly while rockhounding near mines. It only takes seconds to start a chain reaction ending in disaster. A careful and common sense approach to searching the old dumps should not be too eventful though danger has many hiding places. Sure footing is not guaranteed and cannot be trusted to eyesight alone. Tailing piles are often unstable and steep.

ROCKHOUND ETIQUETTE

Most of Wyoming is public land, however much of this wide open space is leased out to the private sector. Ranchers' grazing leases should be of particular concern to rockhounds in this harsh and hard climate that makes virtually every acre count. A small hole thoughtlessly created by shovel or vehicle can quickly erode productive land into a barren wasteland.

Rockhounds are not new to Wyoming. Many sites plainly show just how popular some specimens were. Some of the more popular, heavily advertised treasure areas are now acres of deep hazardous holes that can seriously injure both humans and animals. A rancher's opinion of this goes without saying, so the simple rule for improving cooperative land use relations is to leave the land the way you found it, or as nearly so as possible. It is said of litter, if you can pack a can or bottle in full, you can certainly pack it out empty. The same

These specimens are abundant, but the legal sites for collecting them are not.

applies to filling holes: If you can dig them, you can fill them with less effort than it took to empty them. With many sites already closed due to abuse, a word to the wise should be sufficient. Think beyond today for everyone's benefit.

Always leave gates the way you find them. If it was open—even if it seems wrong—leave it open. In this vast expanse you may find cowboys moving livestock. Keep in mind that both the cowboy and livestock probably have very little company. The reaction of a horse, mounted or not, to a loud horn or exhaust could be disastrous. Park as far out of the way of moving livestock as possible, and shut off your vehicle. Your courtesy will be appreciated, and you could be rewarded with directions to an otherwise unknown area. The proper place to enjoy bucking broncos is the rodeo.

Bureau of Land Management

The BLM defines a rockhound as one who collects rocks, minerals, and fossils as a hobby. Collecting is permitted on all BLM lands with a few restrictions.

Most importantly, the rockhound must not create a significant disturbance. This is a little vague, but common sense tells us that we should not dig to the point where we cause erosion or pollute streams and other water resources. Nor should we drive our vehicles on soft soil where the wheel tracks will create gullies that promote erosion.

Collecting "small" amounts of rock and mineral specimens is allowed, but small is not defined. The idea is to differentiate between recreational collectors and commercial miners, so if you can carry your rock bag to your vehicle, you are probably okay.

Rules for petrified wood are more specific. The limit is 25 pounds per day, per person, not to exceed 250 pounds per year.

:collecting, too, has some special regulations. Except in designated areas, plant and invertebrate fossils may be collected without restriction. Vertebrate fossils, which include those of fish and mammals, may not be collected on BLM lands.

For the latest information on collecting rules in various areas, or for directions or maps, drop in to the local BLM office, or contact the main office in Denver.

USDA Forest Service

Forest Service rules and regulations are essentially the same as those of the BLM. The Forest Service does not have the 25 pound or 250 pound limit for petrified wood, but specifies small quantities. The fossil regulations are the same as the BLM's.

State Lands

Collecting is permitted on state wildlife refuges as long as there is no significant disturbance of the land and the collecting is for hobby purposes.

Road cuts provide some very good collecting and are open, providing that digging does no damage, traffic is not disrupted, and safety is maintained.

Private Property

It is vital to obtain permission before collecting on private property. Owners of farms and ranches are usually generous about allowing those who ask to collect on their property, if it will not interfere with their operations. The real problem is often finding someone to ask. In some cases the owners do not even live in the state. The only way to gain access to such spots is to go to the county recorder's office and try to find a name and address for the owner. This is a time consuming process, but if the site looks particularly good, it might be worth the effort. Please resist the urge to enter the land just because there is no one watching.

In the case of mines on public lands, it is reasonable to assume that if there is no posting and no signs of recent work, it is probably okay to collect. If questions or disputes about access on public lands arise, check it out at the local Forest Service or BLM office.

Where Collecting is Prohibited

Collecting is not allowed in National Parks or National Monuments. Permission is only rarely granted for collecting on tribal lands. The best rule of thumb for determining collecting status is to ask the owner—whether that is a private landowner or a government agency.

YELLOWSTONE

It should go without saying that collecting is not allowed in Yellowstone National Park. Still, the time taken to find and study where and what the specimens are is still a wise investment, and there are plenty of other wonderful features to explore within the park.

Without doubt Yellowstone is Wyoming's strongest calling card. The wonders found within its boundaries are an advertisement in a class of their own. At one time Yellowstone was called "Colter's Hell" after that former Lewis and Clark expedition member reported on its wonders.

Trapper and mountain man Jim Bridger visited the area and also helped spread the fame of Yellowstone's unique features. One story credited to Bridger tells of a petrified bird in a petrified tree singing a petrified song. There are indeed some beautiful petrified trees in the park, but if there were any petrified birds they have all migrated out of the area since he saw them.

Some of the better-known places to view petrified trees are between Tower Junction and Cooke City. Visiting most of the specimens requires an off-road hike, although there is a paved narrow road west of Tower Junction go-

Mammoth Hot Springs is a photogenic masterpiece.

ROCKHOUNDING SITES IN YELLOWSTONE

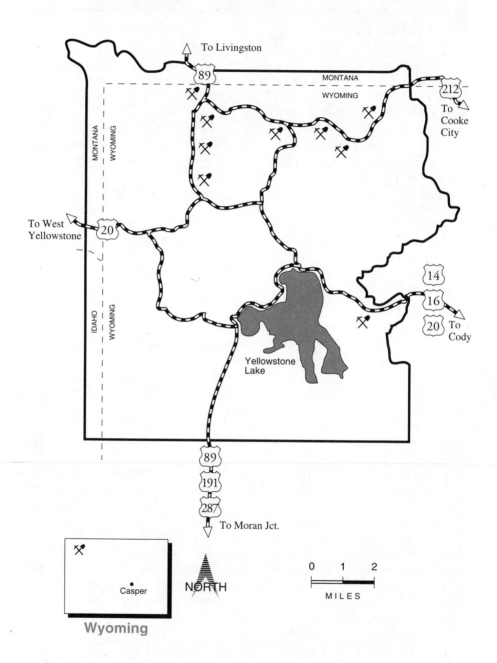

Permanent residents of Yellowstone National Park provide amusement and danger; be alert.

ing south of the road to Mammoth Hot Springs that leads to a petrified tree—but trailers and large vehicles are not recommended,

Specimen Ridge south of Slough Creek holds three tall vertical stumps, within several layers of additional specimens. Indeed, a forest is more descriptive of the large deposit. Hike up Amethyst Mountain from the Lamar River picnic area. Wade the Lamar River and move up the ridge. Keep alert for other specimens and wildlife as you journey up the ridge.

Fossils of marine animals can be observed in the canyon walls along Pebble Creek and in the limestone behind the Pebble Creek campground.

Going south out of Mammoth Hot Springs toward Norris will provide some interesting views. The Sheepeater Cliff will bring the Devil's Tower of northeastern Wyoming to mind.

Obsidian Cliff is just down the road. Another story attributed to Jim Bridger, though the actual author is probably unknown, tells of hunting in the area of the Obsidian Cliff. A hungry trapper spots a nearby elk. Shot after shot neither kills nor alarms the large animal. The trapper soon discovers he was merely seeing the elk through the mountain of glass, and his bullets were just bouncing off of its smooth surface. I am sure you will want to verify this story on your own by visiting the spot.

Top Notch Peak south of the park road in the vicinity of Sylvan Pass also contains petrified wood. The peak is west of Sylvan Pass, which is in turn west of the East Entrance coming from Cody, Wyoming. The specimens are found in volcanic sedimentary rock.

HOW TO USE THIS GUIDE

The sites in this book are divided into five geographic sections: Northeast Wyoming, Southeast Wyoming, Central Wyoming, Southwest Wyoming, and Northwest Wyoming. An overview map of the state is provided near the front of the book to help identify which section would best fit your plans. Each section is then itemized into specific site locations and features. Entries for specific sites are numbered to correspond with the accompanying map.

Site entries adhere to the following format:

Number and name of site.

Land type: General information about the site—mountainous, desert, forested, and other features.

Land manager: Specific departments, agencies, and private designations are listed here. Regulations on collecting certain specimens are different, depending on which agency manages the site. Note the section on Rockhound Etiquette. When collecting rocks and minerals in Wyoming, it is important to be aware of the status of land ownership and mineral rights. This always is subject to change. Mining claims may be filed that overlay known rockhound collecting sites, or on-going legislation may create new wilderness areas that encompass old collecting sites, making it illegal to remove anything from them. When rockhounding in Wyoming, obey all signs regarding current land status and respect all claim markers and no-trespassing signs.

These Sweetwater Agates glow in the dark under an ultraviolet light.

Materials: Specimens known to be found at the site are listed here.

Tools: Helpful tools for convenient specimen collection are listed here.

Vehicle: For purposes of this book a utility vehicle is defined as a high-profile/high-clearance unit. Generally all pick-ups and four wheel drives fit this definition. A few cars and vans will fit this category, depending on the ground clearance of the vehicle. The lower the profile, the greater the risk of being high centered on one of the many abrupt road surfaces. Special restrictions or requirements will also be included in this section.

Accommodations: This includes a general list of amenities available within the closest proximity and approximate mileage from the site.

Special attractions: Interesting, educational, or entertaining features near the site are listed in this section.

Finding the site: Specific site directions begin at easy to identify locations and follow the least confusing routes. Some sites can be reached with less driving, but multiple intersections and lack of landmarks resulted in an alternative route description.

Rockhounding: Pertinent information in regard to weather, access, the best time of year, what to look for, and where to look is recorded in this section.

1   AGATES OF THE MINERAL HILLS

Land type: Pine covered hills.
Land manager: Black Hills National Forest.
Materials: Fossils, agate.
Tools: A carry sack.
Vehicle: Any. Trailers or long vehicles may be difficult to turn around. Other arrangements should be considered before passing the Ranch A Fish Hatchery.
Special Attractions: The Ranch A Fish Hatchery.
Finding the site: Take the Ranch A exit (Exit 205) off of Interstate 90 just west of the South Dakota border. Go south on the well-maintained gravel Sand Creek Road/Forest Road 863 to and through the Ranch A Fish Hatchery. After passing through the hatchery proceed about 4 miles to a bridge where two stream beds meet with the main road bearing to the right or west. There are other forks before this, though the road bears to the left instead of to the right.

Rockhounding: It is a matter here of how many pounds a person wants to carry back to the car. The better pieces seem to come from farther upstream, but the samples sure get heavier when I have to pack them very far. The fossil sponge (as my uncle called it) is dominant for the area and

Looking for keepers in the Sand Creek stream bed.

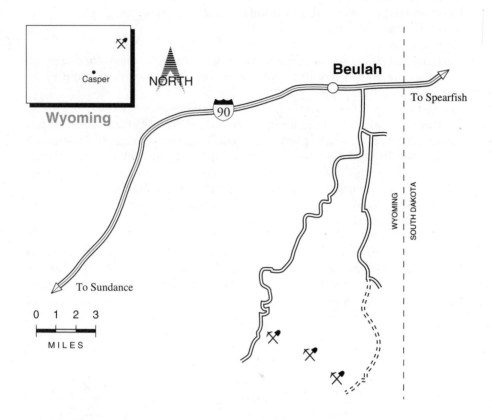

comes in a variety of reds, though they are well rounded from water flow in past floods. If one were to spend the time to find the source, some very fine specimens could be a possibility.

The banded agate looks similar to petrified wood. The yellow, red, and gray banding are layered in different arrangements with pretty uniform size. With some creative slicing, fine pieces can be brought to life.

2   *FLUORITE OF THE BEAR LODGE*

Land type: Pine covered hills.
Land manager: Black Hills National Forest.
Material: Fluorite, limestone.
Tools: Rock hammer.
Vehicle: Any.
Accommodations: Camping, motels, and restaurants within 10 miles.
Special attractions: Devil's Tower.
Finding the site: Take U.S. Highway 14 from Exit 185 on Interstate 90 just west of Sundance. Turn right onto the Warren Peak Road, 1 mile away. Wind your way uphill on this scenic blacktop road for about 5 miles to Forest Road 899 and turn right. Stay to the left on this narrow gravel road for about 0.5 mile to the Ogden Ridge Trail. From here the road is closed to motorized travel, so it is time to warm up the leg muscles.

Rockhounding: The fluorite is found in the limestone along the old road cuts of the trail. It will take some walking to reach the area, but if you remembered your camera and are the sort to appreciate a forest walk it will be a pleasant experience.

There are plenty of pieces to pick up without hammering, though some of the more prized crystals may not be so easily obtained. Copper minerals have been reported at old mine workings, but reclamation has made these sites hard to locate. A specimen or two may remain outside the reclamation area, but the odds are slim.

If you leave this pleasant place in time to view the Devil's Tower a drive along US 14 will offer a more scenic alternative. It could be a welcome change to cruise at a slower pace and drink in the photographic beauty of a backwoods road.

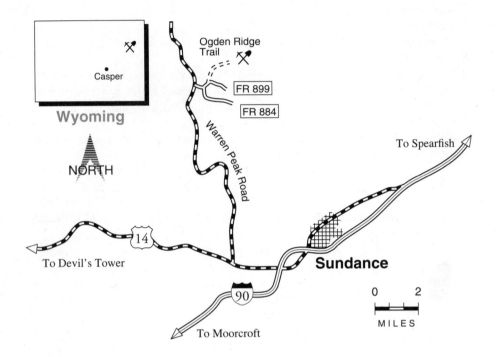

3 FISH SCALES OF PINE RIDGE

Land type: Pine forested prairie ridge.
Land manager: Wyoming Department of Transportation.
Material: Fish scale fossils.
Tools: None.
Vehicle: Any.
Accommodations: Motels and restaurants within 12 miles.
Special attraction: Keyhole Reservoir.
Finding the site: Leave Interstate 90 at Pine Ridge Road (Exit 165). Either side will produce fossils, however the less traveled south side of the exit offers the easiest parking.

Rockhounding: The roadway cuts directly through the Mowry shale, which is the black-colored flat stone. The loose shale laying virtually all over will provide plenty of choices. Some of the well-preserved scales display clear growth rings.

There are other places within the state to find these scales. With a little coaching, kids can scout for additional locations in your travels. It might make the long stretches of wide open country more fun for them.

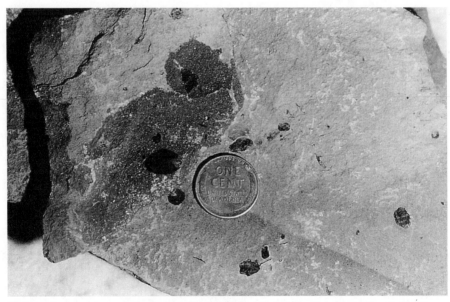

Fish scales require some close-up scrutiny, but their plentifulness will quickly fill a bag.

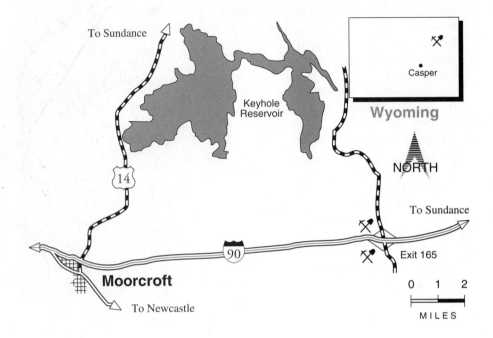

Land type: Badlands prairie.
Land manager: Wyoming Department of Transportation.
Material: Selenite crystals.
Tools: None.
Vehicle: Any.
Accommodations: Motels and restaurants within 20 miles at Buffalo.
Finding the site: Leave Interstate 90 at Schoonover Road (Exit 77) about 13 miles east of Buffalo, or about 47 miles west of Gillette. The site is located in the dark (almost black) gumbo on the south side of the interstate.

Some of the selenite found on the surface at Schoonover.

Rockhounding: The crystals litter the gumbo here. With a little searching some very fine twinned pieces can come to light. Care should be taken in wet weather as the road becomes difficult, if not impossible to travel, and walking through the site itself will produce a very large mess in the car interior upon your return.

Separating the crystal from a partial blanket of black dirt.

4 *SELENITE AT SCHOONOVER*

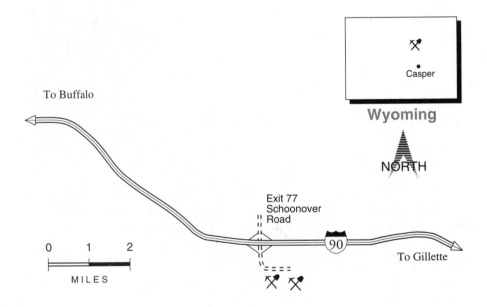

5   DRY CREEK PETRIFIED FOREST

Land type: Badlands prairie.

See Map on page 25

Land manager: Bureau of Land Management.
Material: Scoria, petrified wood.
Tools: None.
Vehicle: Any.
Accommodations: Motels and restaurants within 7 miles at Buffalo.
Finding the site: On Interstate 90 about 7 miles east of Buffalo take Red Hills Road (Exit 65) north to the Tipperary Road. Follow the asphalt Tipperary Road for 5 miles to the Petrified Forest sign. About 0.5 mile of narrow but good road terminates at a turn-around with a gate and a box of informational material.

Rockhounding: No collecting is allowed in the designated area, however the adjoining land is open. There is intermittent private land, which will require permission, so be mindful of fences and signs. The red-capped hills all around are made of the clinkers, and no doubt there is still plenty of wood around as well though it is not as sought after as the agatized wood of other areas.

Upon leaving the site one can drive back toward the interstate, but instead of continuing to the Red Hills exit take the road west back to Buffalo.

Information signs along the Dry Creek Petrified Forest both educate and pinpoint specimens.

It is a fairly well-maintained dirt road and could be slippery when wet. Upon going under the interstate just before getting back to Buffalo, the red scoria will be obviously exposed to your right in unfenced land between the road and I-90.

6   AGATES AND WOOD ALONG HIGHWAY 16

Land type: Badlands desert.
Land manager: Private.
Material: Agate, petrified wood, and fossils.
Tools: None.
Vehicle: Any.
Accommodations: Motels and restaurants at Buffalo within 10 miles.
Finding the site: Take U.S. Highway 16 from Exit 58 on Interstate 90 just east of Buffalo. Travel about 6 miles north toward Ucross.

Rockhounding: The petrified wood, fossils, and agates are in the badland hills on both sides of the highway for the next 10 miles. It is all on private ground and permission is required before any hunting can be done. There are plenty of places to pull in and ask, so if one party is not home the next one might be. Be careful of the dogs—some of them are very protective.

The wood here is not as sought after as the opalized wood of the southwest. All the same it comes in all sizes and for the most part has been left in place. There are some pieces that would require a front end loader and truck to collect.

Fossil plants are a little harder to find. These will be found in the sandstone outcrops sticking out of the sides of the hills. Not all of them have plants, but when you find one, more will follow.

Agates are more prevalent on the ridge tops, though smaller ones pop up along with the petrified wood. More than a few arrowheads have been fashioned out of this type of stone. In places one can still see the teepee rings where the Native Americans stayed. They did not use up all the material for their tools, however. Plenty more untouched pieces are weathering out every year.

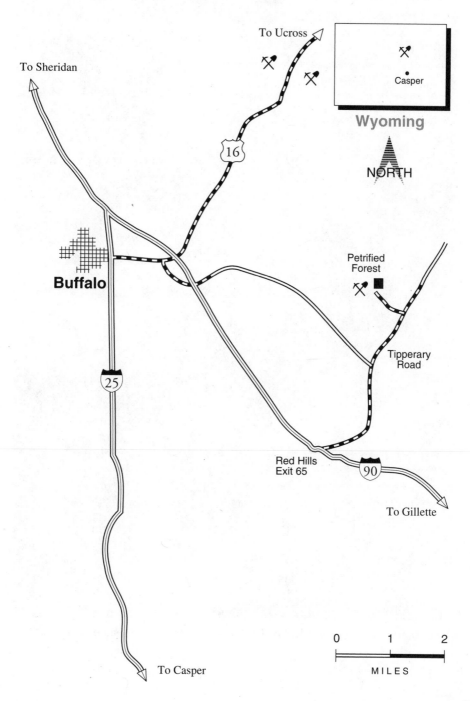

To Ucross

To Sheridan

Casper

Wyoming

NORTH

16

Petrified
Forest

Buffalo

Tipperary
Road

25

Red Hills
Exit 65

90

To Gillette

0   1   2

MILES

To Casper

This petrified tree trunk is 4 feet in diameter with indications of more underneath.

7   SELENITE AT NEWCASTLE

Land type: Badlands prairie.
Land manager: Wyoming Department of Transportation.
Material: Selenite crystals, shell fossils.
Tools: None.
Vehicle: Any.
Accommodations: Motels and restaurants at Newcastle within 5 miles.
Finding the site: Newcastle is about 47 miles south of Sundance on Interstate 90, via Wyoming Highway 585 and US 85. Newcastle also can be reached from Rapid City on US 16. This tour through the Black Hills could include a stop at Mount Rushmore as well. Take US 85 south out of Newcastle toward Lusk. About 1 mile past the four-way stop sign at the US 85/16 intersection, the road cuts expose the deposits.

Rockhounding: The crystals will sparkle in any available light and are easily found along either side of the road. With some careful, persistent searching the twinned samples can be picked up.

Finding fossils will take a little more effort. The red shale seems to hold the most promise. Not all the red shale contains the small, well-defined specimens. The small imprints are easily recognized when spotted. Other discoveries might be awaiting the careful scrutiny of a diligent explorer.

Selenite is recovered from between the sage brush in roadcuts like this one south of Newcastle.

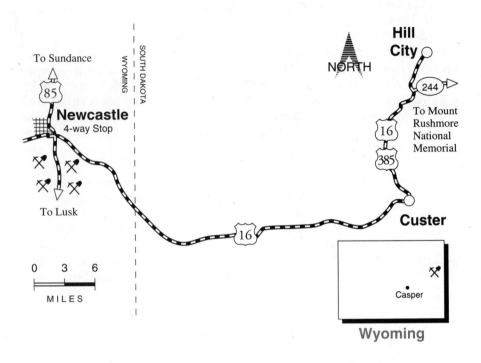

Land type: Prairie.
Land manager: Wyoming State, private.
Material: Chert, limestone, calcite crystals.
Tools: Rock hammer, chisel.
Vehicle: Utility.
Accommodations: Motels and restaurants at Lusk within 5 miles.
Special attractions: The Stagecoach Museum.
Finding the site: Lusk is a small town on U.S. Highway 18/20 about 41 miles east of Orin junction on on Interstate 25 at Exit 126. Just before entering Lusk, there will be some roadside tables on the south side of the highway. Turn right, onto the dirt road at the west end of the tables, before getting to them. If you missed the turn don't panic, simply make use of the turnout at the roadside tables. Don't create a traffic hazard. Go down the dirt road 1.5 miles to the second ranch house on the right. The map shows how to get in and out of the quarry, though a stop at the ranch is advised for permission to enter the site. The actual quarry is about 1.5 miles beyond the ranch house.

Rockhounding: The quarry exposes a variety of layers with multiple beds of chert challenging removal. There is plenty of loose material scattered

Crystals and chert are exposed in the wall of this quarry, with plenty of leftovers in the loose rocks.

about from the previous work if pounding and chipping is not on the agenda. The upper levels could pose a threat from falling rock.

The limestone boulders contain many crystal-lined cavities. The crystals vary in size and clarity, and the better ones always seem to be firmly attached to a huge chunk of stone. This means a certain amount of work is required to acquire selected pieces.

8 *CRYSTALS AT LUSK*

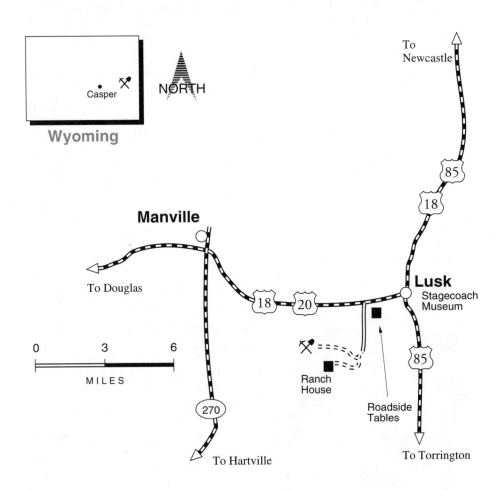

9　HARTVILLE ONYX

Land type: Mountain type badlands.
Land manager: Bureau of Land Management.
Material: Onyx, crystals, agate, jasper.
Tools: Rock hammer, chisel.
Vehicle: Any.

See Map on page 33

Accommodations: Restaurants and motels within 7 miles at Guernsey.
Finding the site: At Exit 92 on Interstate 25 take U.S. Highway 26 about 15 miles east to Guernsey. Go through Guernsey and turn left onto Wyoming Highway 270. Drive to the stop sign in Hartville, about 5 miles farther. At the stop sign turn left and go 1 mile. Take the Guernsey State Park Road to the left for about 1 mile. Follow the blacktop road to where the parallel gravel road splits away to the right. Look for two very rough ruts climbing over a small saddle. Unless you have a four wheel drive and like to tackle rough country, park here.

Rockhounding: About 0.75 mile past the intersection an old quarry is cut out of the hillside. Onyx is scattered within the larger boulders on the top section of this quarry and will require chiseling. There are some loose pieces laying about, but they are often not the most desirable.

If you chose to walk the distance, there are more rewards awaiting you in the washouts along the way. Red jasper and dark moss agate fill in spaces between various crystal displays. Here again a hammer will come in quite handy. Some very large pieces contain very small samples. Be careful when pounding, as the crystal structure could be destroyed by a careless blow. The agate and jasper do not require any pounding, however the agate does tend to hide in a white crusty coating.

Be prepared for some manual labor if you want large pieces of the onyx.

10 GARNETS AT GUERNSEY

Land type: Mountainous.
Land manager: Bureau of Land Management, private.
Material: Garnet, agate.
Tools: None.
Vehicle: Any.
Accommodations: Restaurants and motels at Guernsey within 2 miles.
Finding the site: Guernsey is about 15 miles east of Interstate 15/Exit 92 on U.S. Highway 26. Go through Guernsey and turn left on Wyoming Highway 270 for 0.5 mile. Look for the rock quarry on your left with a barbed wire fence gate. Park safely here.

Rockhounding: It is best to go on foot from here. There is an old road visible from the highway, though it may be on private ground. The garnets, which were previously mined for industrial purposes, will take some searching. All along the ridge is prime hunting ground with the exposed areas of past mining offering the best material.

In your wanderings along the top, you may notice an old agate mine. The mine operated for a long time, and the agates have reportedly been cleaned

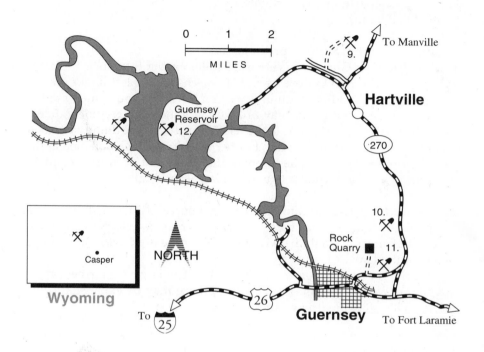

out—so, naturally, every rockhound hopes to find the one magnificent piece that was overlooked.

The mine itself escaped my search, but I found hunting garnets more time consuming than originally planned. If you do happen on the mine, keep in mind that where mining and blasting have altered the native rock structure, unstable and dangerous conditions often exist. Easier, safer agate hunting is available at many other sites.

11 QUARRY COPPER MINERALS

See Map on page 33

Land type: Mountainous.
Land manager: Private.
Material: Copper minerals, crystals.
Tools: Rock hammer.
Vehicle: Any.
Accommodations: Same as previous site.
Finding the site: Guernsey is about 15 miles east of Interstate 15/Exit 92 on U.S. Highway 26. On the east end of Guernsey turn left under the railroad overpass instead of continuing east on US 26. If you come to the intersection for Wyoming Highway 270, you've gone too far. About 0.5 mile away, the quarry office will be to the left. The actual mine dumps are about 0.3 mile past this turn on the left, but permission must be obtained at this office before proceeding. The foreman that can grant permission is there only during normal business hours, so plan accordingly.

Rockhounding: The old mining area is not currently active, but this can change at any time. Unfortunately, there is no real place to park anywhere close to the sites. It would be wise to drive by the area beforehand to get the lay of the land.

Several mine dumps contain the minerals. The largest is farthest away, and has the best selection. In the future, there may be expansion of the quarry that will expose new samples.

Copper minerals are found in many old mine dumps along this narrow draw.

Land type: Reservoir shoreline.
Land manager: Guernsey State Park
Material: Youngite (fluorescing agates).
Tools: Rock hammer, chisel.
Vehicle: Boat.
Accommodations: Restaurants and motels at Guernesy.

See Map on page 33

Finding the site: Guernsey State Park is on U.S. Highway 26 about 14 miles east of Interstate 25/Exit 92. The boat ramp is in the park, which is open year-round. A motorized boat with a good supply of fuel is recommended, allowing more opportunity to explore the ever-changing shoreline.

Rockhounding: The most well-known deposit for youngite is currently closed to collecting. I have excluded the exact location to avoid losing access to other sites because of those who might choose to ignore the closure. Dynamite was used to break the youngite away from cave walls, resulting among other things in some unsafe conditions, not to mention the damage done to the specimens. The message for those of us collecting samples today is to think about those who will follow us. All is not lost, however. The most well-known deposit is not the only one.

Youngite is a combination of drusy quartz and banded agate that can be found encrusting limestone in natural caves and crevices. This agate will flouresce light green in both long-wave and short-wave ultraviolet light, though one does not need to pack in lighting tools to identify these beauties. With careful use of a hammer and chisel, specimens can be recovered with minimal damage to the remaining structure.

Guernsey Reservoir is completely drained every year. The shoreline continually gains size as summer turns to fall. As the reservoir shrinks the opportunities increase for newly uncovered specimens. As with any other reservoir shoreline, be aware of the inconvenience that deep mud can create. Different parts of the cliffs along the shore will be exposed at various water levels. Since the youngite will be found in the crevices of the limestone there is really no time better than another. What is good at one elevation will be too hard to reach, either too high or under water, at other times.

13   GLENDO GOODIES

Land type: Reservoir shoreline.
Land manager: Glendo State Park.
Material: Jade, petrified wood, agate, fossils.
Tools: None.
Vehicle: Any.
Accommodations: Motel and convenience store at Glendo; restaurant at the marina; fee camping at various areas along the reservoir.
Finding the site: Easiest access to Glendo State Park is from Glendo at Exit 111 on Interstate 25. There are multiple access areas to the shoreline including the Sandy Beach area on the opposite side, 15 miles from Glendo.
If you explored the youngite at site 12 and survived with your sanity and your boat, this would be another spot a boat could be useful.

Rockhounding: The best hunting here is when the water is low, usually late in the year (September through November). What you'll find depends on where you hunt, so a stop at the Glendo Rock and Craft shop for advice on likely spots for specific specimens would be helpful.

Fossils seem to be most prevalent along the southern shore or near the red rock. The Sandy Beaches of the northern shore have produced some agate, however this is a very popular area and it is not always easy to find room.

The beaches of Glendo Reservoir offer a recreational and pleasant treasure hunt for jade, agates, petrified wood, and fossils.

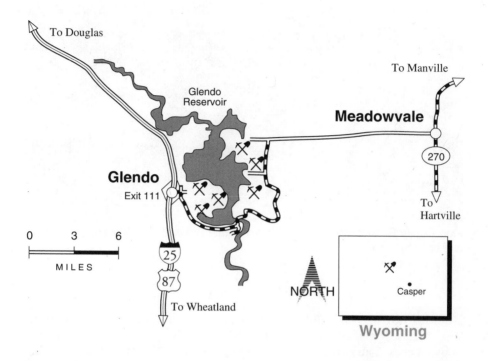

To Douglas

Glendo
Reservoir

To Manville

Meadowvale

270

Glendo

Exit 111

To
Hartville

0   3   6

MILES

25

87

To Wheatland

NORTH

Casper

Wyoming

14   MOSS AGATE ROAD AT DOUGLAS

Land type: Rolling hills.

See Map on page 39

Land manager: Converse County Highway Department.
Material: Agate.
Tools: None.
Vehicle: Any.
Accommodations: Restaurants and motels at Douglas within 25 miles.
Finding the site: At Douglas, take exit 140 off of Interstate 25. Go south to Wyoming Highway 91 and turn right. Turn left 3 miles down this road at the junction with Wyoming Highway 96 to stay on Wyoming Highway 91. Proceed 14 miles on WY 91 to Converse County Road 15. Turn right on Moss Agate Road/CR 15 and drive to the ridgetop about 2 miles away.

Moss Agate Road follows the top of Moss Agate Ridge shown between the fence and horizon

Rockhounding: The multicolored agates here are frustrating to collect. There are few places to park on the road and private land owners may not allow access. The roadbed itself contains plenty of booty, but obstructing traffic to hunt for them can cause problems and conflicts. As property ownership changes, better conditions could develop.

Most of the pieces picked up along the road were small and heavily chipped. Some bigger ones were found, but none large enough to slab. Tumbler material seemed to be all there was available. The drive is a pleasant variation from the high-speed interstate, but the improved dirt road could be a real test of skill when wet.

14   MOSS AGATE ROAD AT DOUGLAS

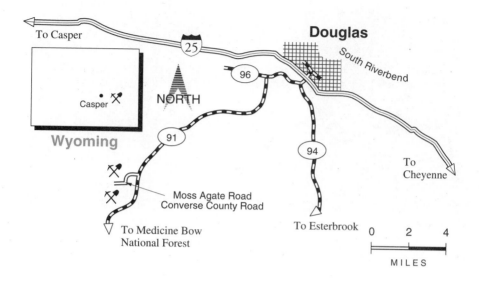

15   NATRONA ARCHERY RANGE AGATE

Land type: Pine covered mountain.
Land manager: Natrona County.
Material: Agate (banded chert), iron pyrite, feldspar.
Tools: Rock hammer and carry bag.
Vehicle: Any.
Accommodations: Motels, campgrounds, and restaurants within 10 miles and a county campground at the site itself.
Special Attractions: Tate Earth Science and Mineralogical Museum, Fort Caspar, and Rose's Rocks and Gifts.
Finding the site: Take Wyoming Highway 258 from either the Interstate 25/Exit 185 in the east, or Wyoming Highway 220 from the west. Wyoming Highway 251 intersects WY 258 just south of the main part of Casper, roughly halfway between. Start marking the mileage at this intersection.

Agate is scattered all along the ridge tops in the Natrona County Archery Range.

Go south on WY 251 for 6 miles to the Hogadon Ski Area turnoff and turn right. Follow the Archery Range signs as they direct you through this populated area for the next 3 miles. The last few miles of this stretch turn to gravel and degenerate to one-lane dirt. When arriving at the range turn toward the campground, though one could park anywhere out of the way.

Rockhounding: The blue-gray agates are laying pretty much all over with certain areas also producing crystals. Some of the better pieces show excellent banding. The pyrite crystals seem most prevalent on top of the knolls, though more exploration could turn them up in other locations.

This is an active archery range so pay attention to signs and heed restricted areas. There is a three-day camping limit at the time of this writing with adequate hiking a safe distance from the feathered shafts. Don't cross any fences without first asking permission. There are plenty of people living up here and they do not take kindly to uninvited entry. There is plenty of collecting area on public land.

On your way out you will pass an active mine on the right. A portion of the roadway is a reclaimed pit that has some very inviting sparkles. The Pacer Corporation of Custer, South Dakota, has warning signs at the gate, but there is plenty of unposted area, too. I am not sure whether this area is open to collecting.

NATRONA ARCHERY RANGE AGATE— MUDDY MOUNTAIN AGATE— CASPER ALABASTER

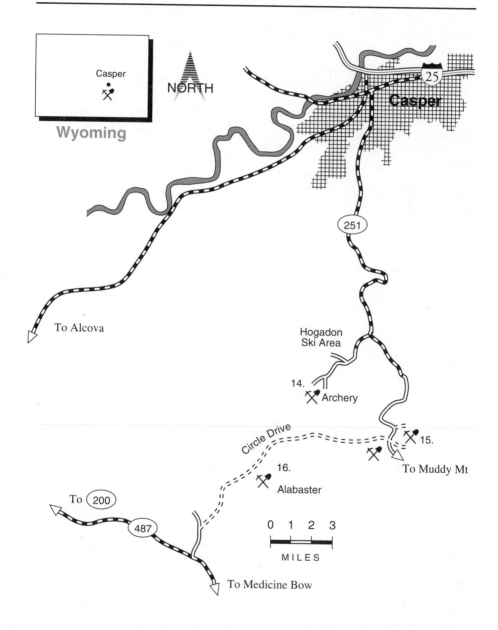

Casper

Wyoming

NORTH

Casper

25

251

To Alcova

Hogadon
Ski Area

14.
Archery

Circle Drive

16.
Alabaster

15.

To Muddy Mt

To 200

487

0 1 2 3
MILES

To Medicine Bow

16 *MUDDY MOUNTAIN AGATE*

Land type: Desert mountain draw.
Land manager: Bureau of Land Management.
Material: Red agate.
Tools: Rock hammer (optional).
Vehicle: Any.

See Map on page 41

Accommodations: Motels and restaurants within 18 miles at Casper. Campgrounds and RV parking available at various points in between and about 5 miles past the site on Muddy Mountain.

Finding the site: Take Wyoming Highway 258 from either the Interstate 25/Exit 185 in the east, or Wyoming Highway 220 from the west. Wyoming Highway 251 intersects WY 258 just south of the main part of Casper, roughly halfway between. Follow WY Hogadon Ski Area 6 miles away. Stay to the left on Circle Drive/County Road 505 for about 4.5 miles to a cattle guard. The road will degenerate from asphalt to dirt toward the end, though it is well used. After crossing the cattle guard, continue down the hill and start looking for two parallel ruts leading along one of the narrow ridges. Turn in here if it is not muddy and park.

Rockhounding: There are fragments of red banded agates with white spots of differing intensity in the washes. Along the edge of the rim there

Smaller, easy to find red agate is recovered from ruts like this productive site at Muddy Mountain.

are bigger pieces, though the ugly crust can make them difficult to identify. Take your bag along. The distance back to the car can grow surprisingly fast as your eye catches more productive possibilities and entices you on.

The fragments along the washes and road cuts are mostly tumbler pieces. The harder-to-find bigger ones offer some slabbing potential. There may be more on the west side of the road, though we found plenty on the east side.

17 CASPER ALABASTER

Land type: Badlands.
Land manager: Bureau of Land Management.

| See Map on page 41 |

Material: Gypsum and agate.
Tools: None.
Vehicle: Any.
Accommodations: Motels and restaurants within 33 miles at Casper.
Finding the site: Go west of Casper on Wyoming Highway 220 toward Alcova. At Wyoming Highway 487 go south 8.6 miles to Circle Drive/ County Road 401. Mark your odometer here. The site is 3.8 miles from this point just across a cattle guard with a battered BLM sign to your left. Stay

White alabaster is easy to identify in contrast with the red shale along Circle Drive.

to your right coming from this direction when the road changes to Circle Drive/County Road 505. This site can be reached from the Muddy Mountain sites as well, though the dirt road could be muddy and an impassable nightmare. Check locally to determine the status of the road.

Rockhounding: The gypsum is obvious all along the horizon. The white rock stands out in stark contrast to the red shale it lays on. Weathering has exposed plenty of pieces of various sizes for you to choose from. These unique stones are an excellent carving medium that even younger children can work with.

Pieces of red agate much like the ones found at the Muddy Mountain site are littered among the sage brush. These seem to appear at random and can add a pleasant benefit to the dusty trip up here.

18   MOSS AGATE RIDGE

Land type: High prairie.

See Map on page 46

Land manager: Bureau of Land Management
Material: Moss Agate and agate.
Tools: A rock hammer and carrying bag.
Vehicle: Any.
Accommodations: Motels and restaurants within 60 miles.
Finding the site: Go west of Casper on Wyoming Highway 220 to Wyoming Highway 487. Turn left, and go south for about 31 miles. The road will climb out of badlands terrain onto a flat plain. When you see the Lone Tree Road/BLM Road 3141 start looking for a turnout with a wide cattle guard to your right, not quite 2 miles farther on. There are other gates, but the road across the cattle guard makes it much easier. After crossing the cattle guard you can go either direction along the old highway, though an abandoned quarry is to your left.

Rockhounding: Small but very nicely wind-polished moss agates lay all over the flats here. When first turning off the main highway you can go to the left and in a short distance a small gravel pit will offer some excellent opportunity. Every storm erodes more of the beauties out, and the quarry provides plenty of exposure for the weather to work on.

A rock hammer or some other type of pry bar is very helpful in the hard crusty ground. Don't pass up a small agate thinking it unworthy. Larger treasure may be hiding beneath it though most of the pieces are tumbler-size material. These stones have a natural luster, however, that makes tumbling optional and makes them easier to spot.

Wind-polished moss agate pops up in various distances along the vast Moss Agate Ridge of the Shirley Basin.

19 SILICIFIED WOOD OF MARSHALL

Land type: Rolling desert hills.
Land manager: Bureau of Land Management, private.
Material: Petrified wood.
Tools: None.
Vehicle: Any.
Accommodations: Motels and restaurants within 40 miles.
Finding the site: The site is located 7 miles east of Wyoming Highway 487 along the Shirley Basin Road. Go west of Casper on Wyoming Highway 220 to WY 487. Drive an additional 5 miles past Moss Agate Ridge (site 18), for a total of 36 miles on WY 487 to the Shirley Basin Road/Carbon County Road 2. Turn left onto this improved dirt road and go 7 miles.

Rockhounding: The silicified wood is found on both sides of the road for the last 2 miles. Most of the better pieces seem to come from the roadside ditches. With a little effort and time some real beauties could come out of the deeper ones. Don't forget the limit of 25 pounds per day.

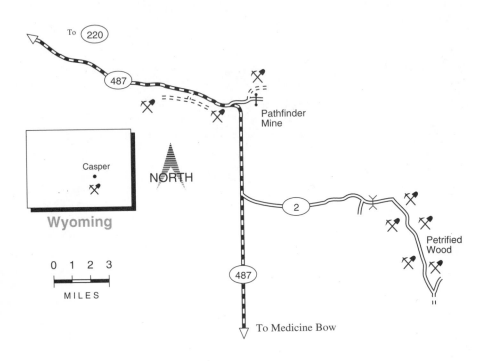

To (220)

487

Pathfinder
Mine

Casper

NORTH

Wyoming

0 1 2 3

M I L E S

2

Petrified
Wood

487

To Medicine Bow

Looking for larger samples in a recently exposed road cut.

Land type: Desert prairie.
Land manager: Bureau of Land Management and private.
Material: Petrified wood and agate.
Tools: None.
Vehicle: Any.
Accommodations: Motel and restaurant within 25 miles at Medicine Bow.
Finding the site: Little Medicine Road/BLM 99 is 17 miles north of Medicine Bow on Wyoming Highway 487. If you are coming from Casper, Little Medicine Road/BLM 99 is about 5 miles past the second junction with Wyoming Highway 77 on WY 487. Follow the gravel Little Medicine Road/BLM 99 to the north for 6.2 miles to Walker Draw Road/BLM 3136. Park safely, paying attention to ground condition.

Rockhounding: Agates are the most common finds on these flats, which offer a variety of wind-polished samples. The black and white wood that is most desired is more difficult to find, which makes its discovery even more delightful. Don't forget to look up from time to time. Distance and direction become muddled in the quest of prize pieces and you may find yourself farther and in a different direction than you thought from your vehicle.

Most of the pieces here are easily picked up off the surface. A few will need a little help, but its best not to dig. Grazing is prime use for this land, and local ranchers—who pay for the grazing rights on the public land—do not appreciate damage to the land that could reduce the quality and quantity of feed produced in this harsh environment. Access to the BLM land requires crossing these ranchers' property. Future access will depend on maintaining friendly, cooperative relationships with them.

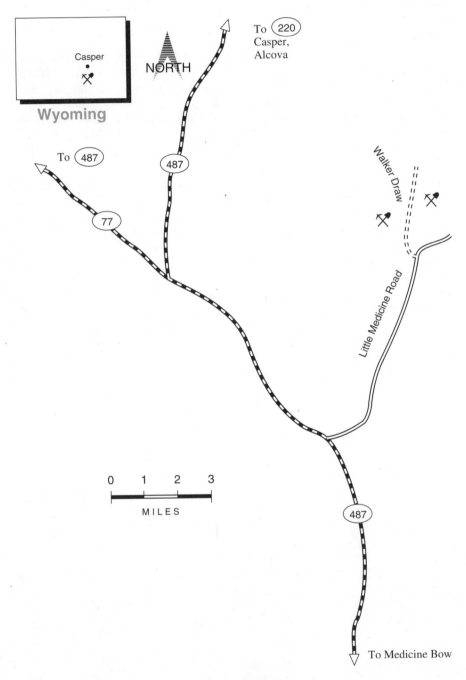

Casper

Wyoming

NORTH

To 487

77

487

To 220
Casper,
Alcova

Walker Draw

Little Medicine Road

0   1   2   3
MILES

487

To Medicine Bow

Land type: Rolling prairie hills.
Land manager: Bureau of Land Management and private.
Material: Petrified, agatized, and some opalized wood.
Tools: None.
Vehicle: Utility.
Accommodations: Motels and restaurants within 15 miles in Saratoga.
Finding the site: The site is 14.5 miles south of Walcott on Interstate 80/ Exit 235 on Wyoming Highway 130. At the Platte River Pick Bridge Road/ County Road 508 prepare to turn left opposite the county road. You will need to open and close a gate. Drive along with respect for the conditions and minimizing any damage to the grazing. Proceed to one of the hilltops and park in a safe way.

Rockhounding: The wood is found on the ridge tops, where the weather reveals its hiding places. Be forewarned that this area is aggressively guarded by overly zealous individuals who have claimed that they own this public land and threatened rockhounds with prosecution for trespass. If you would feel more comfortable with a local guide, Bill, the owner of Castro's Rock Shop in Encampment can arrange that, and can also suggest other local hotspots.

Don't forget—you can only collect 25 pounds of petrified wood in a day, and no more than 250 pounds in a year.

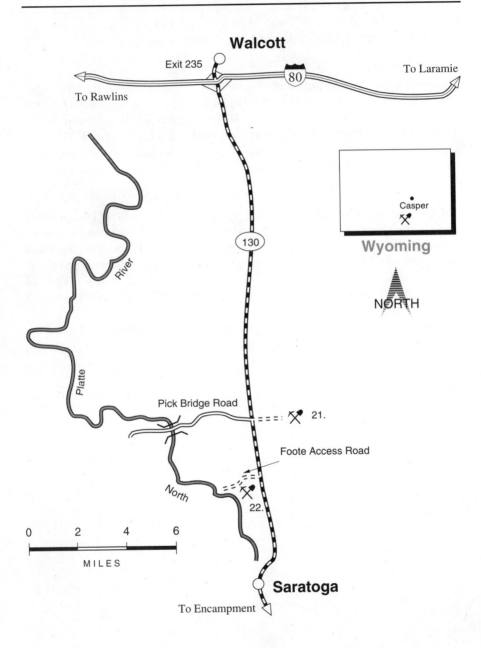

Land type: River breaks.
Land manager: Bureau of Land Management, private.
Material: Moss agate, agate, petrified wood.
Tools: None.
Vehicle: Any.
Accommodations: Motels and restaurants within 13 miles in Saratoga.
Finding the site: The Foote Public Access Road is 2.5 miles past the Platte River Pick Bridge turnoff or 17 miles south of Interstate 80/Exit 235 on Wyoming Highway 130. Go west on the dirt Foote Road for 1 mile to the parking area.

Rockhounding: As you drive along the narrow road a cut will drop through some nice agate just before a cattle guard. This may be private, but there is no need to worry as there is plenty to pick from in the abandoned quarry ahead.

The public access is predominantly for rafters and fisherman, but a few motorcyclists make the trip as well. Unless you need shade, it is better to park away from the river. That way you will not be blocking access to the water, and, as a reward for your consideration, you will not have to carry your treasure as far. In any case, we did not find much of interest in the river rock.

Agate is sometimes hidden in variety of disguises, like this piece.

Land type: Mountainous.
Land manager: Bureau of Land Management, private.
Material: Mica, garnets, crystals.
Tools: Rock hammer (optional).
Vehicle: Utility.
Accommodations: Motels and restaurants at Encampment and Riverside within 5 miles.
Special attractions: Grand Encampment Museum, Castro's Rock Shop.
Finding the site: Take Wyoming Highway 70 through Encampment to the last house on the left. Turn left on a well-traveled dirt road and follow this over a small creek and through a narrow cattle guard to the junction of the Encampment Trailhead/Road 3407. Turn to the right and go on up the hill about 1 mile. Look for a faintly visible car track to your left. Turn onto this old road and park.

Rockhounding: The piles of rock are the remains of a past mining venture. Be careful—there my be hard-to-see holes that can be dangerous.

There are plenty of sparkly specimens to choose from here. Garnets are present but it takes a trained eye to see them. Before coming up here a stop at Castro's Rock Shop would be well worth the time. Bill may even be up for a field trip, but even if he's not, the samples displayed there and at the museum will provide inspiration and give you an idea of what to search for.

Mine dumps like the one in the center of the picture can be found most anywhere in these hills near Encampment.

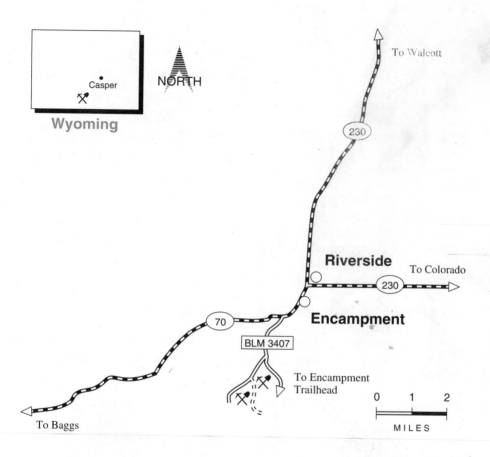

To Walcott

230

Riverside

To Colorado

230

70

Encampment

BLM 3407

To Encampment
Trailhead

To Baggs

Casper

Wyoming

NORTH

0   1   2

MILES

Land type: Badlands desert.
Land manager: Bureau of Land Management, private.
Material: Agate, moss agate, jasper.
Tools: Rock hammer, bag, water (canteen).
Vehicle: Utility.
Accommodations: Motel and food within 45 miles.
Special Attraction: Como Bluff Dinosaur Dig, Como Bluff Fish Hatchery.
Finding the site: Take U.S. Highway 287/30 west out of Laramie for 44 miles. Turn right onto the Marshall Road (Albany County Road 610) and travel north on this improved dirt road for 35 miles. Old log cabins may still be standing in the distance on your left as the 35th mile rolls up on your odometer. There is a well-maintained fence that serves as a landmark if the cabins are gone. Find a safe place out of the way to park.

See Map on page 56

Banded moss agate is one of the treasures tempting seekers to endure the long dirt road to Marshall.

If you're coming from the west you will find the Marshall Road 13 miles east of Medicine Bow. Medicine Bow is on US 287/30, 38 miles east of Walcott at Interstate 80/Exit 235.

Rockhounding: The agates are on the flats and require some footwork. A lot of distance can be covered in a short time and water is not readily available. It is essential to pack in your own water in this country, and it would be wise to bring a lunch as well. It's a long way to town.

The red-tinted agate you'll find here will look best when cut and polished. The finished products are well worth the extra time to pick out select samples. The rock hammer will come in handy, though use it with caution to avoid destroying an otherwise perfect piece.

Miles of wide open country offer some solitude near Marshall.

25 HOLIDAY ROAD AGATES

Land type: Badlands desert.
Land manager: Bureau of Land Management.
Material: Agate, jasper.
Tools: Rock hammer (optional), bag.
Vehicle: Utility.
Accommodations: See previous site.
Finding the site: Take U.S. Highway 287/30 west out of Laramie for 44 miles. Turn right onto the Marshall Road (Albany County Road 610) and travel north on this improved dirt road for 36.5 miles, going past site 24 to the Holiday Road intersection. Turn left onto the Holiday Road and go 1.6 miles. Find a safe place to park off of the road. There can be a fair amount of traffic in spite of how desolate it looks.

Rockhounding: The selection here is wind polished and easy to spot. A rock hammer or other prying device might be useful in separating a stubborn piece. With the abundance of material to choose from it is not necessary to spend a lot of time working at it. If any amount of time is spent in the area there will be little room for hauling the payload.

  With some searching, a beautiful sort of banded moss agate can be

MARSHALL MOSS AGATE—
HOLIDAY ROAD AGATES

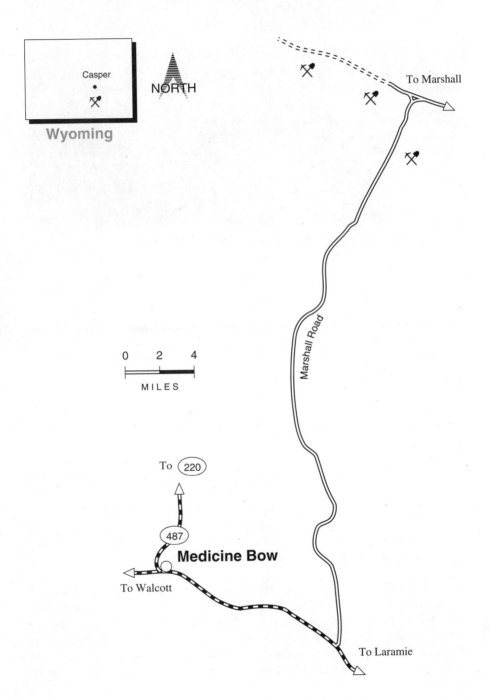

Casper

Wyoming

NORTH

To Marshall

Marshall Road

0   2   4
MILES

To (220)

487

Medicine Bow

To Walcott

To Laramie

Holiday Road divides a long flat agate bed for a distance that tries one's endurance.

discovered. It is finds like this that keep a person looking well past time to move on. Keep in mind that this can be harsh country, and when thunder storms paint the horizon, it is time to get out.

Continuing down this dirt road one is likely to find agate all along. A more defined moss agate without the banding appeared between sage brushes 4 miles further. Most of the agates here were tumblers. Some searching along the rim farther to the south might turn up larger specimens. Allow yourself plenty of time here—it is well worth it. Plan to arrive early, or to camp out for adequate treasure hunting.

Overview—Central Wyoming

Jade is without doubt the most searched for prize of the central Wyoming area. Many fine gem pieces have come from this vast expanse. Though hunted extensively for many years, significant discoveries are still made to this day. Erosion, both natural and man-made, uncover new specimens to reward the persistent eye of a dedicated hound.

A great deal of walking is required to properly cover the fields. Dedicated hunters take food and water to enable them to search an entire day, without returning to their vehicle.

The wind seems to always blow in this high desert prairie, which can make even a sunny day chilly. The dry dusty air makes it easy to empty a canteen in very short time. With long distances between services, it is necessary to do some serious planning. When your belly is empty and your tongue sticks to the roof of your mouth it is not comforting to know the nearest store is 50 miles away.

26 COTTONWOOD CREEK DINOSAUR TRAIL

Land type: Badlands.
Land manager: Natrona County Park.
Material: Fossils.
Tools: None.
Vehicle: Any.
Accommodations: Motels and restaurants within 25 miles.
Finding the site: The Alcova store is west of Casper on the south side of Wyoming Highway 220 about 8.5 miles west of the junction with Wyoming Highway 487. At the store turn left off of WY 220 onto Natrona County Road 407. Follow this blacktop road for 6.3 miles to the gravel Cottonwood Creek Road. Turn right and go a little more than 1 mile to the Cottonwood Creek Dinosaur Trail.

Rockhounding: Collecting of fossils is not allowed here, but this site offers an excellent education for future use. As you work your way along take notice of the type of terrain and color of rock. Then look into the distance across the Alcova Reservoir and make a mental note of the geology. The same formations are present on the other side of the lake.

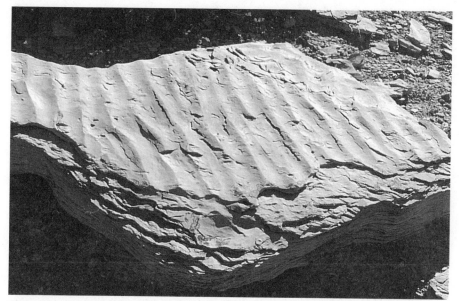

This piece of beach is too hard for sandcastles now, but samples like this make good yard additions.

26-27 *COTTONWOOD CREEK DINOSAUR TRAIL—PELECYPODS OF ALCOVA*

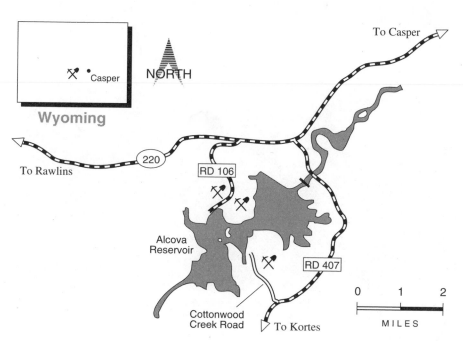

Land type: Badlands.
Land manager: Natrona County.
Material: Fossils.
Tools: Rock hammer.
Vehicle: Any.
Accommodations: See previous site.
Finding the site: After leaving the Cottonwood Creek Dinosaur Trail go back to Wyoming Highway 220 at the Alcova store. Turn left on WY 220 and go about 4.5 miles to Natrona County Road 406 toward the Alcova Lake Park. Follow this road about 3.5 miles through the colorful road cuts to pull outs along the left side of the road. It might be easier to actually go past these and turn around below and thus not go against the fairly steady traffic.

Rockhounding: The fossils here are not as easily found as in the Cottonwood Creek site. However, their plentifulness is astounding. At the first spot the entire creek bed is made up of pelecypods. A rock hammer will be most useful in separating smaller pieces from the otherwise too heavy ones.

Farther on toward the marina the road cuts through a fossil bed of belemnites and pelecypods. The collecting here is a little frustrating as it is

Alcova Reservoir divides the geologic formation which includes the Cottonwood Creek Dinosaur site on the other side.

so close to the road. Do not dig at all, since the loose material left behind will become a major problem whenever this area gets any moisture. With a little effort there is plenty to be found without disturbing any of this.

Now that you have learned a little geology, you will know what to scout for. Use the knowledge of formations presented here to seek out similar deposits. There are many of them throughout the state, some of which are as yet undisturbed. Remember that collecting vertebrate fossils is not allowed on public lands. There are plenty of other fossils to collect. As a general rule, surface collectibles are abundant enough to avoid digging. Besides, who likes shovel work anyway?

28   LEO JADE

Land type: Badlands, mountainous.
Land manager: Bureau of Land Management, private.
Material: Black jade, agate.
Tools: None.
Vehicle: Any.
Accommodations: Motels and restaurants within 30 miles at Casper. Store and gas at Alcova with some camping.
Finding the site: The Alcova store is west of Casper on the south side of Wyoming Highway 220 about 8.5 miles west of the junction with Wyoming

Jade can be found most anywhere in this vast territory, though most hounds search near the base of the granite outcrops.

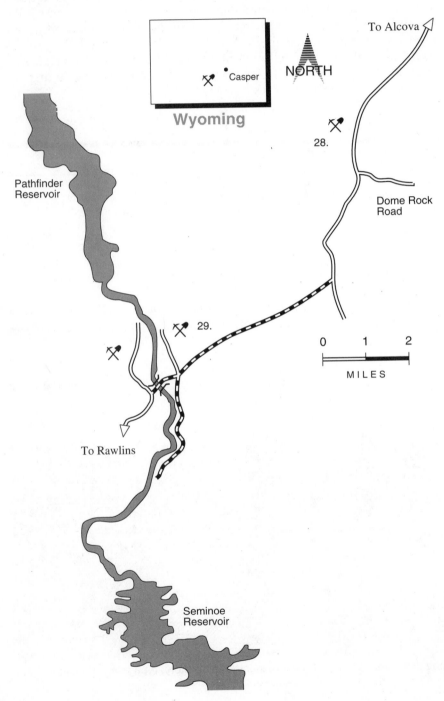

To Alcova

NORTH

Casper

Wyoming

28.

Dome Rock
Road

Pathfinder
Reservoir

29.

0   1   2

MILES

To Rawlins

Seminoe
Reservoir

Highway 487. At the store turn left off of WY 220 onto Natrona County Road 407. Follow this blacktop road south for about 21 miles to Dome Rock turnoff. Stay on CR 407 and begin looking for a safe and convenient place to leave the road to the west.

Rockhounding: This is a hard place to search. There is so much area and a lot of time can be spent looking with little or no results. The black jade here can be difficult to distinguish from ordinary country rock. Many a "wannabe" has come from long hours of searching. For the persistent, a fine piece of gem quality jade makes it all worth while. If you have not hunted for jade it would be wise to stop at a rock shop and study the "rough" samples they have. The Alcova Store sometimes has some samples for sale that could be useful.

There is a long ridge running pretty much north to south and the better hunting seems to be along its edges. There are always stories of new jade being found. Constant weathering brings new resources to light for observant searchers.

A major drawback of this area is the difficulty of hunting only for jade when agate is easier to find. I have been told that once I pick up an agate I am done hunting for the elusive jade. My agate pile is considerably larger than my little jade pile, so I would have to admit this is true, at least for me.

29 KORTES NEPHRITE

Land type: Badlands river bottom.
Land manager: Bureau of Land Management, private.
Material: Jade, agate.
Tools: None.
Vehicle: Any.
Accommodations: Motels and restaurants within 45 miles at Casper.
Special attractions: Fishing in the blue ribbon waters of the North Platte.
Finding the site: The Alcova store is west of Casper on the south side of Wyoming Highway 220 about 8.5 miles west of the junction with Wyoming Highway 487. At the store turn left off of WY 220 onto Natrona County Road 407. Follow this intermittent paved and gravel road for 34 miles to the Sage Creek Road. Turn to the right on this gravel road and go to one of the parking areas along the river.

Rockhounding: This is another of the areas that can take a lot of effort for little results. Depending on how important it is to find jade, this may not be worth the trip for just rockhounding. The river is well known for the fishing and perhaps both activities will appeal to you. With luck, you might you might end the day with more than one kind of catch.

Some excellent fishing is available below Kortes Dam for those who tire of the maddening hunt for jade.

There are some large holes, made by heavy equipment at some point in the past, that could offer real rockhounding advantages. Bright red-banded material in these holes that came to light every now and then distracted me, however, and when I found these, my search for jade ended.

Land type: Badlands prairie.
Land manager: Bureau of Land Management.
Material: Jade, agate, jasper.
Tools: None.
Vehicle: Any.
Accommodations: Restaurants and motels at Casper within 45 miles. RV parking at Alcova Lake Park within 21 miles.
Finding the site: Drive west of Casper on Wyoming Highway 220 past the Alcova Lake Park turnoff. Continue another 18 miles west on WY 220 to the Dry Creek Road (Natrona County Road 321). Turn to the right on this gravel road and go 4 miles. Turn off to the right onto the deeply rutted, soft sand trail and go to the granite rocks. Find a safe out-of-the-way place to park. Take heed that the ground is soft, and it doesn't have to rain to get you stuck in some of this country.

Rockhounding: As mentioned in the overview, this is a vast area to hunt in. The agate seems to be more prominent in the exposed areas of the small hills. Jade is the hardest to look for and the most elusive. The olive green variety in this area can turn up just about anywhere, though the edges of the granite outcrops seem most promising.

Olive green jade has been found in plenty along the outcrops like this in the past.

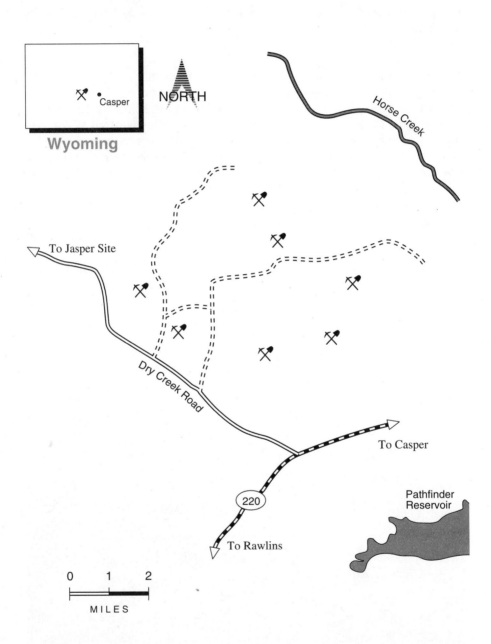

31   DRY CREEK JASPER

Land type: Badlands prairie.
Land manager: Bureau of Land Management, private, Natrona County Highway Department.
Material: Jasper.
Tools: None.
Vehicle: Any.
Accommodations: See the previous site.
Finding the site: Drive west of Casper on Wyoming Highway 220 past the Alcova Lake Park turnoff. Continue another 18 miles west on WY 220 to the Dry Creek Road (Natrona County Road 321). Turn to the right on the Dry Creek Road and go 21 miles on this gravel to improved dirt road. Park along the road side.

Rockhounding: The dark red jasper is found mostlly in smaller pieces here. The easiest place to discover these shiny pieces is along the road cut itself. There is some private land here that is not well marked so respect the fences and other property line markers.

Scattered in and around the rock outcrops one can occasionally pick up larger pieces of jasper. These are more difficult to spot than the broken ones

Bald Mountain is one of the landmarks contrasting the skyline along Dry Creek Road.

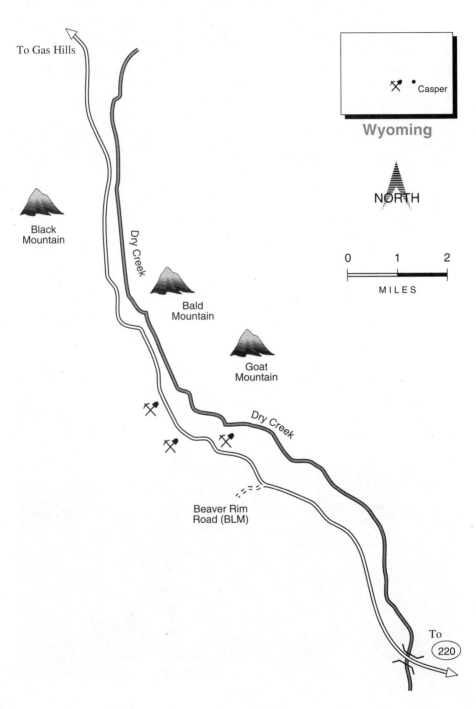

To Gas Hills

Black
Mountain

Dry Creek

Bald
Mountain

Goat
Mountain

Dry Creek

Beaver Rim
Road (BLM)

Casper

Wyoming

NORTH

0   1   2

MILES

To
220

at the roadside. Their size makes the search more worthwhile for those who use cutting and polishing tools to capitalize on the hidden beauty of these stones. If land ownership cannot be determined, stick to the road—there is plenty of material there for the finding.

32   BUZZARD ROAD JADE

Land type: Badlands prairie.
Land manager: Bureau of Land Management, private.
Material: Jade.
Tools: None.
Vehicle: Four wheel drive recommended.
Accommodations: Restaurants and motels at Casper within 60 miles, depending on how far into the prairie you drive.
Finding the site: Buzzard Road/Natrona County Road 410 is 1 mile west of the Dry Creek Road of the previous sites on Wyoming Highway 220. This dirt road can become a test of driving ability and patience within a very short distance. A stop at the Alcova store might produce some up to date information on both the condition of the road and tips on hotter hunting locations. The farther away from the main road the better the odds.

Rockhounding: This area covers more area than can be hunted in several days, much less a brief vacation stop. If you plan to work this area for the dark olive to black jade it would be wise to visit with some of the locals. The Alcova store is a good place to start, though various rock shops usu-

Buzzard Road is a road in name only when it's wet.

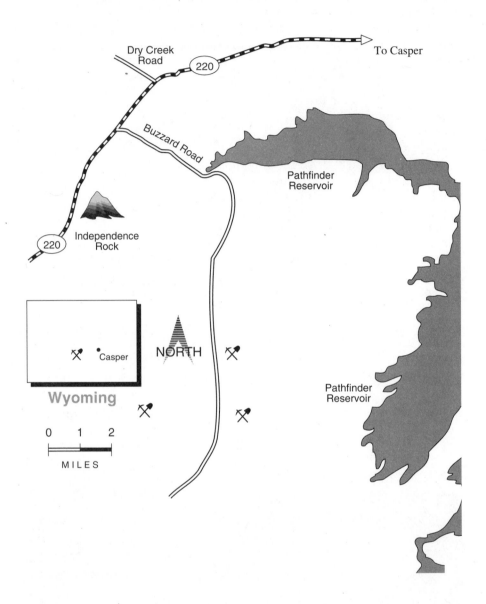

ally are helpful as well.

There are plenty of granite-like outcrops all around this area, but reaching them can eat up a lot of time, so plan accordingly, and take plenty of water and food. Hunger pains and a dry mouth can destroy the thrill of any discovery in a very short time.

Land type: Rocky desert.
Land manager: Bureau of Land Management.
Material: Sweetwater moss agate, jade.
Tools: Shovel, pick, and bucket.
Vehicle: Utility.
Special attractions: Climbing around the granite rocks adjacent to the site, ammunition clips and .50 calibur brass can still be found. During training of fighter pilots during the World War II days, the granite formations represented enemy battle ships. With a little imagination one can see these rock "ships" afloat in the vast expanse of an uninterrupted sage "sea."
Finding the site: At Three Forks turn off of Wyoming Highway 220 onto U.S. Highway 287/Wyoming Highway 789 and drive north for 17 miles. If you are coming from Lander, the Agate Flats Road will be 7 miles east of Jeffrey City/Home on the Range on US 287/WY 789. Turn right onto the Agate Flats Road/BLM Road 2404 and continue down this dirt road for 9 miles. Toward the end of the 9 miles a ranch will appear off to your right. Stay to the left on the less used road and continue over the rocky crest. When you see some stock tanks on the left you are at the beginning of the Agate Flats.

Rockhounding: These smaller agates are more commonly tumbled for a full polish. An interesting and attracting feature to these particular specimens is the light green color seen when they are exposed to short-wave ultraviolet light.

This site has been known since about the turn of the century. Agates were at one time hauled by wagon to the railroad at Rawlins and then shipped as far as Germany. The agates are less abundant now, but not gone. The more desirable ones are the darker moss agates, though there are also yellow opaque agates in the area. Plan on digging—it is possible to find an overlooked specimen on the surface, but it is unlikely.

For those with jade fever and a good deal of energy the outer edges of the flat hold the most promise. The better pieces seem to come from the edges of the rock outcrops mentioned in the special attractions. Where desert meets granite, and erosion tears away the overburden, some olive green jade has been recovered. This area does not seem to be hunted as hard as others and just might produce adequate material with a smaller investment of time.

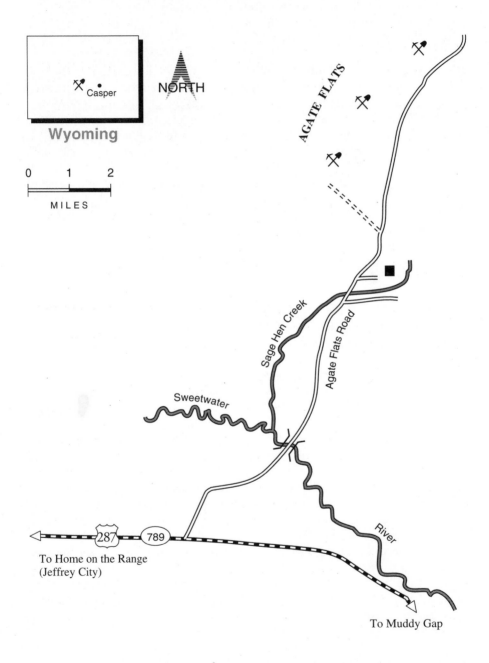

The agate beds stretch almost to the horizon in this windy country.

34   GAS HILLS BLACK JADE

Land type: Rocky desert.
Land manager: Bureau of Land Management.
Material: Jade, agate.
Tools: Rock hammer (optional).
Vehicle: Any.
Accommodations: Limited services at Jeffrey City (Home on the Range), Motel/store/cafe at Muddy Gap within 24 miles, restaurants and motels at Lander within 60 miles.
Special attractions: The Oregon Trail runs parallel with the Sweetwater River through this area. Along the cliffs in selected spots pioneers carved their names and their date of arrival in the stone. Most of this is on private ground and permission must be granted.
Finding the site: Jeffrey City/Home on the Range is 57 miles southeast of Lander on U.S. Highway 287. An old gas station is on the north side of the highway, in fact it is the only gas station on the north side. Go north on the wide gravel road that runs by this gas station on the east side. Travel 4 miles down this road, over the Sweetwater River, and across a cattle guard. Park well off the road and prepare to hike.

Rockhounding: The black jade found here is covered with the rusty red

Black jade has been found along the road side here with new pieces coming to light from erosion every year.

rind that makes it difficult to identify. The best searching seems to be at newly eroded sections or a freshly bladed road. The jade does seem to come with more quartz inclusions, similar to the Microwave Towers jade, but good quality pieces have been reportedly found here.

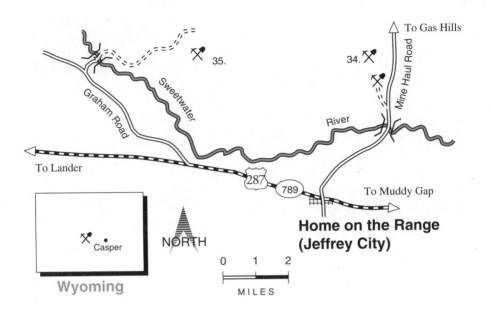

Home on the Range (Jeffrey City)

Wyoming

Casper

NORTH

0   1   2

MILES

To Gas Hills

To Lander

To Muddy Gap

35.

34.

Mine Haul Road

Graham Road

Sweetwater

River

287   789

35   *MICROWAVE TOWERS SNOWFLAKE JADE*

Land type: Rocky hills, desert.
Land manager: Bureau of Land Management.
Material: Jade.
Tools: Rock hammer.
Vehicle: Utility; large vehicles and RVs are not recommended.
Finding the site: Leaving Jeffrey City/Home on the Range, travel west on U.S. Highway 287/Wyoming Highway 789 for 6 miles. Turn to the right onto the Graham Road and go 4.5 miles to the second road and turn right again. The county road goes directly through the Graham ranch complex after crossing a narrow bridge to the other side of the Sweetwater River. It is not necessary to stop at the house, however it is generally appreciated, and you can check on current conditions at the same time. Proceed on up this now narrow and rough road for 6 miles to the upper country.

Rockhounding: Be careful of the still active jade claims in this area—green stakes or posts mark the boundaries. The tall towers to your right are the microwave towers referred to in local conversation and the site's name.

Snowflake jade is found among these rock formations near the Microwave Towers.

There is plenty of territory to hunt for jade here without violating the active claims.

The dark green jade here is called snowflake jade because of the quartz inclusions. These inclusions are generally considered undesirable, so many samples are available to persistent searchers and one can at least take home some form of jade. These pieces are mostly located in and around the granite outcrops dominating the area.

Gem quality rubies have been reported from this area. A mining claim is given the credit, though there is always hope that another sample or two will be discovered outside the boundaries of private workings.

36   APPLE GREEN JADE OF HOME ON THE RANGE

Land type: Mountain, desert.
Land manager: Bureau of Land Management.
Material: Jade, agate, jasper.
Tools: None.
Vehicle: Any.
Accommodations: Restaurants and motels within 50 miles at either Lander or Riverton.
Finding the site: Bison Basin Road is 20 miles west of Jeffrey City/Home on the Range and within sight of Sweetwater Station on U.S. Highway 287/ Wyoming Highway 789. Turn to the south on this dirt road and proceed as far as desired.

Rockhounding: Local rockhounds know the hot spots for the sought-after apple green jade. Almost all of the apple green seems to come from the south side of U.S. Highway 287. It has been found in a very large area including the distant Crooks Mountain south of the highway. Even if you aren't guided to a special hot spot by a local rockhound, recent or future erosion could reward a hunter's diligence with a new productive site.

Careful searching produces what are called slicks—semi-polished pieces that are easy to identify in a rock shop display, but difficult to spot in the field. The large amount of wind-polished agates often prove too tempting to pass up, and gem quality jade can easily be overlooked.

Apple green jade is still being found between here and Crooks Mountain in the horizon.

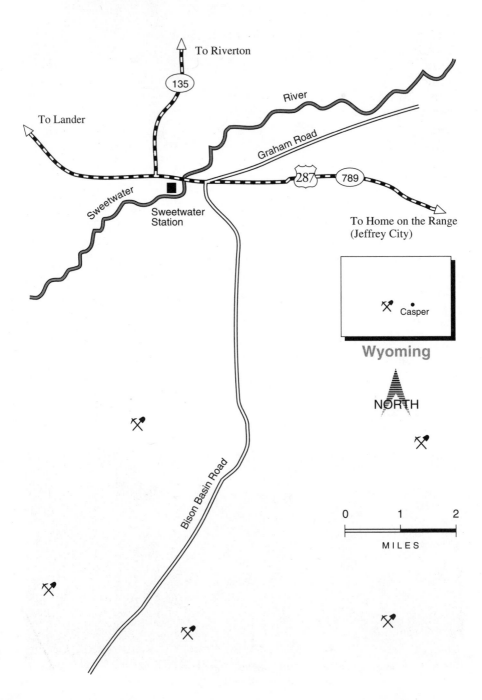

Land type: Badlands desert.
Land manager: Bureau of Land Management.
Material: Agate.
Tools: None.
Vehicle: Any.
Accommodations: Restaurants and motels at Riverton within 31 miles.

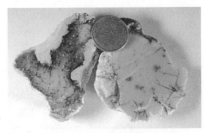

Sliced samples of dendritic agate from Cedar Rim.

Finding the site: Sweetwater Station is about 37 miles southeast of Lander on U.S. Highway 287/Wyoming Highway 789. At Sweetwater station turn to the north on Wyoming Highway 135. Cedar Rim Road/BLM Road 2301 is 7 miles north of this intersection. Turn to the right onto this improved dirt road and travel about 1 mile to the top part of the ridge.

If you are coming from Riverton on WY 135 the Cedar Rim Road will be 10 miles south of the Sand Draw/Wyoming Highway 139 intersection.

Rockhounding: After a long hard search for jade it is pleasant to have a more relaxed hunt. On both sides of the road—and in the road itself—there are various sizes of a unique agate. The dendritic white-to-ivory colored nodules are well worth the small amount of time it takes to find them.

These pieces need to be sliced and polished to display their hidden qualities. With a careful search and a little experience with slabbing, some choice agates can be found here.

Agate nodules litter the Cedar Rim Road bed.

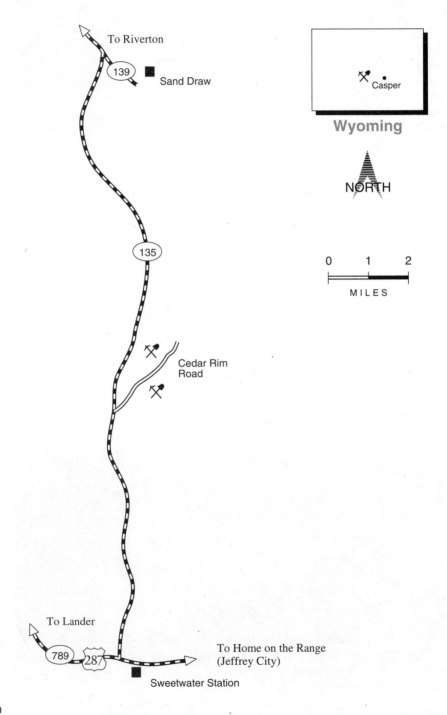

To Riverton

139   ■ Sand Draw

Casper

Wyoming

NORTH

0   1   2

MILES

135

Cedar Rim
Road

To Lander

789 287

To Home on the Range
(Jeffrey City)

■ Sweetwater Station

Land type: Desert.
Land manager: Bureau of Land Management.
Material: Agate, quartz.
Tools: None.
Vehicle: Any.
Accommodations: Motel, cafes, and convenience stores at Farson within 12 miles.
Finding the site: Farson is 40 miles north of Rock Springs on U.S. Highway 191. At Farson take Wyoming Highway 28 for 12 miles to the east toward Lander. If you are coming from Lander, the Tri-territorial Road will be about 65 miles southwest on WY 28. Turn to the south onto the Tri-territorial Road and go down this improved dirt road for about 1 mile to an abandoned railroad bed.

Rockhounding: This area takes some walking and some desire to explore. The agates seem to be the easiest to spot on the exposed knoll tops. It is a dark brown sort of agate or possibly even jasper with a variety of well-rounded quartz scattered about.

As with so many of the sites in this area, this would be considered an alternative area when your wood quota is met. Some exploration could provide excellent conversation pieces as well as beautiful scenery. Don't forget your camera.

Tri-territory Road accesses more than one site with these hills offering some nice quartz.

TRI-TERRITORY QUARTZ—PALM WOOD WEST OF OREGON BUTTES —AGATIZED ALGAE IN THE WOOD BED —EDEN VALLEY PETRIFIED WOOD

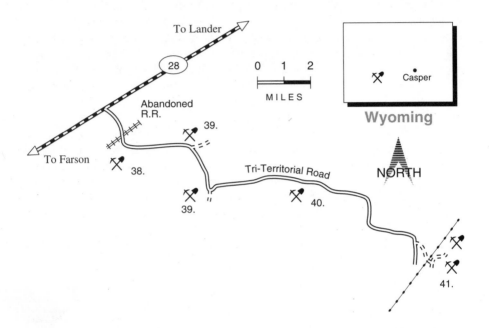

To Lander

28

Abandoned R.R.

To Farson

38.

39.

39.

Tri-Territorial Road

40.

41.

0 1 2

MILES

Casper

Wyoming

NORTH

Land type: Desert.
Land manager: Bureau of Land Management.
Material: Petrified wood, opal.
Tools: None.
Vehicle: Any.
Accommodations: Motel, cafes, and convenience store at Farson.
Finding the site: Farson is 40 miles north of Rock Springs on U.S. Highway 191. At Farson take Wyoming Highway 28 for 12 miles to the east toward Lander. If you are coming from Lander, the Tri-territorial Road will be about 65 miles southwest on WY 28. Continue down the Tri-territorial Road for about 4 miles to the first intersection marked with a directional sign and find a place to park safely.

Rockhounding: There is wood virtually all over this area though most of it is concealed under the sandy soil. Walking along the dry washes provided some beautiful specimens of palm wood. Some careful searching and footwork could locate the source. At the next sign, 1.8 miles farther down the road at an intersection, there is another type of petrified wood. The road cut itself can offer some of the best opportunity, especially if it has been recently graded.

Palm wood specimens found west of Oregon Buttes on the Tri-territory Road.

Along the rims small pieces of wind-polished opal contrast with the otherwise drab country rock. The palm wood seems to be pretty hard to spot, so picking up a handful of opal helps to keep the momentum up. Just as you think there is no more, an especially good piece will jump into sight and energy levels will climb to peak performance once again.

Take time to periodically drag your eyes away from the search to get a bearing on your vehicle. It takes very little time to get a long way, especially when that bare patch just ahead has a promising gleam.

40 AGATIZED ALGAE IN THE WOOD BED

Land type: Desert mountain.
Land manager: Bureau of Land Management.

See Map on page 82

Material: Agatized algae.
Tools: Rock hammer (optional).
Vehicle: Any, but long vehicles or trailers would be difficult to maneuver.
Finding the site: Farson is 40 miles north of Rock Springs on U.S. Highway 191. At Farson take Wyoming Highway 28 for 12 miles to the east toward Lander. If you are coming from Lander, the Tri-territorial Road will be about 65 miles southwest on WY 28. Continue driving down this improved portion of the Tri-territorial Road for about 9 miles. When you top a short flat stretch just before climbing another steeper grade find a safe parking spot. Depending on road conditions, the best place may be to the side of the road itself.

Rockhounding: The surface to your right is littered with a crusted type of agatized algae. It will take some careful study to avoid passing over the good ones. A few will offer a window that reveals an opaque mixture with red billows, or inclusions. Some of the pieces may need to be sliced before knowing for sure. I mention sliced here as opposed to chipped with a hammer. Some very special samples have been ruined with a misguided tap. However, if it is a long way home it might be the best way to avoid packing a dud.

There is a possibility of more petrified wood along the edges or the flats below. At the time I penetrated this field my quota on wood did not allow me any more. It is too difficult for me to choose, since each piece is special. So rather than risk giving into to temptation I stayed with the agatized algae.

41   EDEN VALLEY: PETRIFIED WOOD

Land type: Desert mountain (windy).
Land manager: Bureau of Land Management.

See Map on page 82

Material: Petrified wood.
Tools: None.
Vehicle: Utility, four wheel drive recommended.
Finding the site: Farson is 40 miles north of Rock Springs on U.S. Highway 191. At Farson take Wyoming Highway 28 for 12 miles to the east toward Lander. If you are coming from Lander, the Tri-territorial Road will be about 65 miles southwest on WY 28. Follow the Tri-territorial Historical Site signs for about 13 miles from WY 28. At the top, turn left onto a deeply rutted dirt road just before the Tri-territorial Loop Road. Bounce along and hang on for the next 0.5 mile until passing under the power lines, then go left for about 0.3 mile.

Rockhounding: The petrified wood is all over the surface. There does not seem to be as much opal in comparison to the other areas. The wind-polished pieces are easily seen in the almost barren places between sage brush and sparse grass.

This area does not seem to be hunted hard. Perhaps the road conditions and fast-changing weather make it unattractive. If it does rain, wait for the wind to dry things out. Storms can be seen coming for a great

Solitude and scenery can be welcome partners in this wood bed along the Tri-territorial loop.

distance, but they are fast and furious and arrive more quickly than you would expect.

This is an excellent place to camp. If you are equipped for it, and choose to spend the night, a chorus of howling coyotes may serenade you to sleep. Be aware of lightning hazards in the thunderstorm season.

Wild horses still race the wind across this wide unfenced country. If you look sharp, you may spot them.

42   OPALIZED WOOD OF THE BIG SANDY

Land type: Badlands desert.
Best season: Late summer, early fall.
Land manager: Bureau of Land Management.
Material: Opalized wood, agate.
Tools: None.
Vehicle: Utility, with four wheel drive most desired.
Accommodations: Motel, cafes, and gas within 15 miles at Farson.
Finding the site: Turn off of Wyoming Highway 28 at the Bridger Wilderness Big Sandy Entrance/Farson 4th West, 2.3 miles east of Farson to the Fossil Fish Diggings. The next 11.5 miles of gravel will gradually turn to improved dirt road as it makes its way north. Pass straight through two four-

A fish from the Farson Fish Bed, which is a critical part of the directions to the Big Sandy wood site.

OPALIZED WOOD OF THE BIG SANDY— BIG SANDY ALGAE

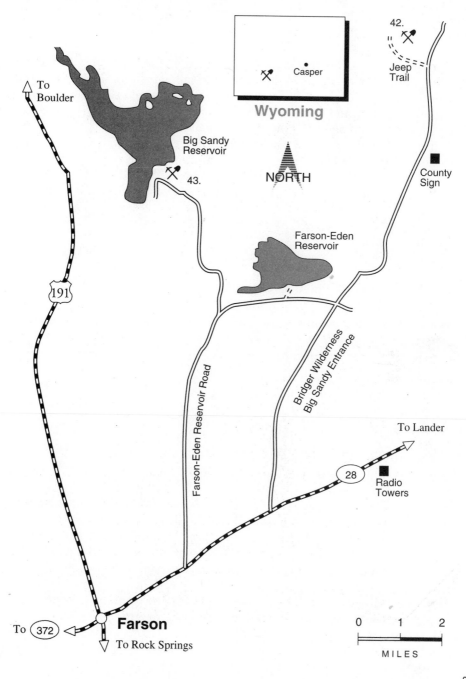

42.

Jeep Trail

To Boulder

Wyoming

Casper

Big Sandy Reservoir

County Sign

NORTH

43.

Farson-Eden Reservoir

191

Farson-Eden Reservoir Road

Bridger Wilderness Big Sandy Entrance

To Lander

28

Radio Towers

To 372

Farson

To Rock Springs

0   1   2

MILES

way intersections. At the first, a house sets in the northeast corner and the second will have a sign proclaiming the Farson-Eden Reservoir Road. When the 11-mile mark rolls into place start looking to the left for tell-tale piles of yellow to rusty brown flat rock. A BLM warning sign will also help spot the place. Now that you know where the fish are, go back toward Farson and look carefully for a hard-to-see intersection with a little-used dirt track going east and west. Follow this dirt track to the west about 1 mile to a stock dam (usually dry).

Rockhounding: The best pieces of wood come from the crest of a small rise to the northeast of the stock dam. Just walking with a sharp eye to the ground will produce a plentiful supply of both opalized wood and opal. It will not take long to fill a sack with the limit of 25 pounds so careful selection is a must. Some of the pieces will show only a small tip peeking out of the blanket of sandy soil so a walking stick with a hoelike end could be useful. Naturally when I first start looking every piece is a keeper, so the stick comes to use after several bendovers.

It might be possible to dig in select places and discover the really big ones, but so far I'm satisfied with the surface samples, and digging would damage the delicate topsoil. Any damage we do will affect our future ability to collect rocks here.

If you meet your wood quota before it is time to leave, there are also agates and opal scattered here and there. The hard part is finding more wood and choosing which to keep and which to leave.

43 BIG SANDY ALGAE

Land type: Desert reservoir.

See Map on page 87

Land Manager: Bureau of Land Management.
Material: Fossil algae.
Tools: Rock hammer.
Vehicle: Any.
Accommodations: See Opalized Wood of the Big Sandy.
Finding the site: Farson is 40 miles north of Rock Springs on U.S. Highway 191. Go 2.3 miles east of Farson on Wyoming Highway 28 to the Bridger Wilderness Big Sandy Entrance (Farson 4th West). Travel down this gravel road to the second four-way intersetion and turn to the left onto the Farson-Eden Reservoir Road, about 5 miles away. Go 2.3 miles on this gravel road and take the right-hand roadway at the unmarked intersection. Follow this improved dirt road 5.5 miles to the dam.

Rockhounding: Erosion leaves fossil algae exposed both on the shoreline and in the banks. Most pieces are large and will require some adjusting for transport. Some of this material will polish well, and, with creative slabbing, add a unique showpiece to any collection.

Fossil algae caps the banks of the Big Sandy Reservoir.

44 THE BLUE FOREST OF GREEN RIVER

Land type: Desert badlands.
Land manager: Bureau of Land Management.
Materials: Opalized wood, opal.
Tools: Shovel, picks, and optional rock hammer.
Vehicle: Utility.
Accommodations: Gas and convenience store at Fontenelle within 18 miles.
Finding the site: Farson is about 77 miles southwest of Lander on Wyoming Highway 28. Beginning at Farson continue on WY 28 to the southwest for 21.3 miles to Sweetwater County Road 8. If you are coming from Interstate 80 take Exit 83, west of Green River, to Wyoming Highway 372. Drive 27 miles north on WY 372. Turn to the right onto WY 28 and drive 6.7 miles to CR 8. Travel north on this gravel road for 11.3 miles. After a long straight stretch you will climb a little rise for the last part of this section. Turn to the right on a worsening dirt road and mark your odometer. You will pass a small rock quarry to your left and some oil field-related turnouts that obviously terminate within sight. At the 2.7 mile mark on your odometer turn to the right on a much narrower dirt road. Stay to the left for about the next 2 miles. This will wind around to a sort of flat top with piles of rock scattered throughout the brush. Find a place to pull safely off the roadway.

Opalized wood from the Blue Forest.

Rockhounding: The Blue Forest is probably the best known site among wood collectors. It has been worked extensively and covers quite a bit of area. If you plan to uproot any of the prize specimens from the unmerciful soil take your lunch. It may not seem far to the Fontenelle store, but the time grinding over the gravel (or dirt) to get there could make a long day of the short mileage.

Take a little time to explore the region and get a feel for just where the digging begins or stops. In the process several broken pieces will invite at least a look. For the most part the opalized wood is encased in a type of algae and may look vaguely familiar. A rock shop will generally have some excellent specimens of wood from this area with the outer crust visible.

For those unwilling or unable to dig, there are plenty of beautiful leftovers. Discarded opal crusts that previous collectors separated from their prizes are easily found. The opal is pretty enough for me to pack home, and when wood is attached to it that makes it all the better.

A pick is helpful in breaking new ground, but use it with caution. A good share of the broken pieces left behind, if not all of them, are there because of this tool. All the more reason to plan ahead and arrive with plenty of time to plot your course of action. The rewards can be well worth it.

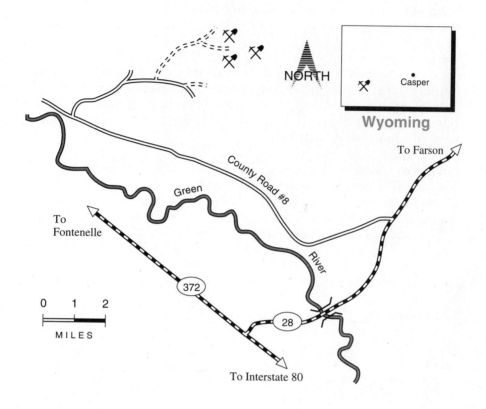

NORTH

Wyoming

Casper

To Farson

County Road #8

Green

River

To
Fontenelle

372

28

0   1   2

MILES

To Interstate 80

45 MUDDY CREEK AGATES

Land type: Desert ridge top.
Land manager: Bureau of Land Management.
Material: Agate, jasper.
Tools: None.
Vehicle: Any.
Accommodations: Motels and restaurants at Fort Bridger within 25 miles.
Finding the site: Take Wyoming Highway 412 north from the Carter exit (Exit 39) of Interstate 80. Go 8 miles north, passing through Carter. Just after leaving Carter look for and turn onto a dirt road to your left. Drive along this road to a parking spot.

Rockhounding: Smaller agates of all types of color are easy to spot, but material for slabbing is harder to find here.

The further from the main road, the better the hunting. It is a dirt road with some potential hazard for conventional cars, so use common sense.

The ridgetops on either side of Muddy Creek could offer some additional collecting. If you have the time and a spirit of adventure it could be a rewarding treasure hunt. There is always the possibility of finding a relatively unworked area of your own. The quantity of material here should last for a very long time—probably well beyond my lifetime.

Agates dominate the rock strewn ridge above Muddy Creek.

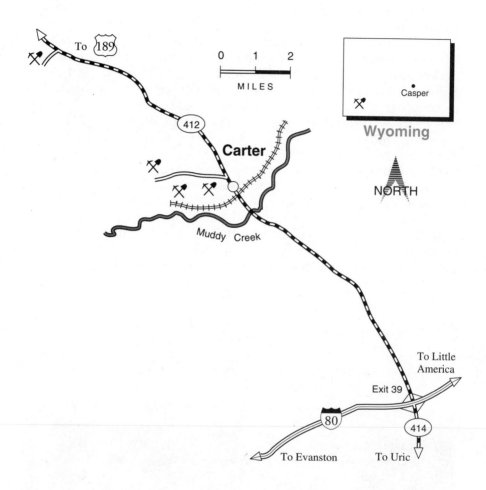

To 189

0   1   2
MILES

Wyoming

Casper

412

Carter

NORTH

Muddy Creek

To Little America

Exit 39

80

414

To Evanston

To Uric

Land type: Badlands.
Land manager: Bureau of Land Management.
Material: Limestone nodules.
Tools: None.
Vehicle: Any.
Accommodations: Motels and restaurants at Fort Bridger within 25 miles.
Finding the site: Go north from the Interstate 80 Carter exit (Exit 39) for 15 miles on Wyoming Highway 412. (If you stopped to load up on agate at the Muddy Creek site continue north on WY 412 for 8.3 miles.) Turn left onto a narrow gravel road and cross the cattle guard. Proceed along this road for 0.7 mile to the edge of the ridge.

Rockhounding: The nodules appear to be encasing some type of formation. These could actually be leftover remains of burned out wood entombed in the ashes and solidified.

    The nodules are found in the white gumbo toward the bottom of the ridge. Apparently the weather erodes them away and leaves them openly displayed along the exposed areas. They will not polish, but they are a curiosity and an excellent conversation piece. It is a pleasant change of pace from the overabundant agate.

Nodules erode from these white-colored deposits along Wyoming Highway 412.

47   *LONETREE BLACK AGATE*

Land type: Badlands.
Land manager: Bureau of Land Management.
Material: Flint, fossils.
Tools: None.
Vehicle: Any.
Accommodations: Motels and restaurants at Mountain View within 25 miles.
Finding the site: Mountain View is about 6 miles south of Interstate 80/Exit 39 on Wyoming Highway 414. Continue south on WY 414 toward Lonetree for about 13 miles. For the next 9 miles, the badlands are capped with goody-filled gravel on both sides of the road. Several well-maintained roads lead to oil field-related equipment and offer fairly easy access.

Rockhounding: Anywhere there is predominantly red gravel exposed there will be flint. This can be a busy thoroughfare, so be thoughtful of traffic. Keep in mind that the roads leading to oil tanks and other related items are not necessarily public—respect and good sense can prevent major problems and road closures.

The color of the flint seems to vary by location. The darker material is more abundant near Lonetree, while the lighter color flint seems to pop up

A variety of sizes will provide the hound with multiple decisions in the Lonetree area.

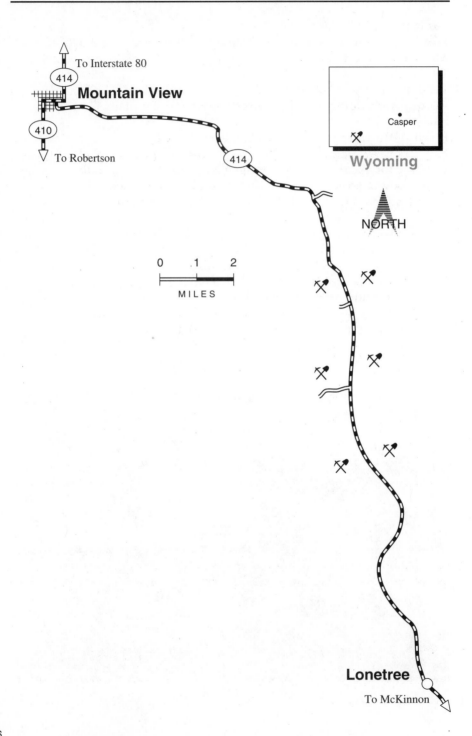

To Interstate 80

414

Mountain View

410

To Robertson

414

Wyoming

Casper

NORTH

0   1   2

MILES

Lonetree

To McKinnon

frequently on the Mountain View side. Most have white spots of various sizes imbedded in different shades of black to purple. There is some cloudy opaqueness.

While here don't overlook the fossils, the most talked about being turtle shell. There are undoubtedly other fossils in the area too, but remember that collecting vertebrate specimens is illegal. I haven't found any myself— I always start out looking for the elusive turtle shell, and return with an overloaded pack of slab material. It is extremely easy to run out of room for any additional material when the picking is this good.

48   AGATE OF BURNTFORK ROAD

Land type: Badlands.
Land manager: Bureau of Land management.

See Map on page 99

Material: Agate.
Tools: None.
Vehicle: Any.
Accommodations: Motels and restaurants within 30 miles at Green River.
Finding the site: The site is 27.5 miles south and west of Green River. At the McKinnon Road, about 18 miles south of Green River on Wyoming Highway 530, turn right. Travel down this narrow blacktop road to the well-marked Burntfork Road/BLM 4315, 9.2 miles away. Turn off to the right here and find a suitable parking spot.

Rockhounding: Here as with most of the other sites in agate country it is a process of selection. The agates here are of the black variety and smaller. They make good tumbler material or cabochons.

If you prefer larger material, pass this site by for the next two sites listed. This could be a pleasant stop on the return trip, and these smaller specimens can fill the space between the bigger pieces you collect elsewhere— if your vehicle is equipped to handle the weight.

49   RED AGATE OF CEDAR MOUNTAIN

Land type: Badlands.
Land manager: Bureau of Land Management.

See Map on page 99

Material: Agate.
Tools: Rock hammer.
Vehicle: Any.
Accommodations: Motels and restaurants within 35 miles at Green River.
Finding the site: At about 18 miles south of Green River on Wyoming

Red agate is mixed with the other rocks dominating these ridges.

Highway 530 turn to the right on the McKinnon Road. Drive 14 miles and turn to the right onto an unmarked but good gravel road . Drive down this road about 3 miles to the edge of a small draw.

Rockhounding: Agates are probably anywhere you want to look. I found the ridge edges the most appealing for larger slabbing pieces. As with other areas of the same formation the most prevalent color is black. In addition to the abundant flint there are vivid red nodules that provide truly inspiring samples.

The red agate may take some looking, though it tends to come in groups. When you find one, take time to carefully survey the surrounding area. A rock hammer comes in handy in prying the sometimes large nodules from the crusty ground.

The badlands formation to the west is a temptation all its own. The road here is reported to go all the way to the top of Cedar Mountain and could offer some real potential for other treasures. There are turtle shells found in the nearby area, probably from the badlands type terrain. If you want to explore for fossils it might be best to do so before picking up any agate so you don't run out of room or damage your vehicle's shocks.

Be careful not to enter private land without asking permission first. A good rule of thumb in this area is if there is a fence do not cross it, and do not go through any gates.

AGATE OF BURNTFORK ROAD— RED AGATE OF CEDAR MOUNTAIN— BANDED FLINT OF MCKINNON

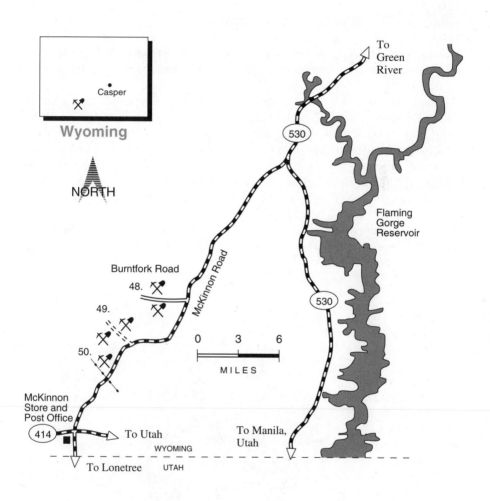

Casper

Wyoming

NORTH

To
Green
River

530

Flaming
Gorge
Reservoir

Burntfork Road

48.

McKinnon Road

49.

530

50.

0   3   6

MILES

McKinnon
Store and
Post Office

414   To Utah

To Manila,
Utah

WYOMING

To Lonetree   UTAH

Land type: Badlands.
Land manager: Bureau of Land Management.
Material: Flint, jasper, agate.
Tools: None.
Vehicle: Utility, four wheel drive advised.
Accommodations: Motels and restaurants within 40 miles at Green River.
Special attractions: The McKinnon country store is an excellent place for coffee and conversation. The first fur-trapper rendezvous in the Rocky Mountains were near here in 1825.
Finding the site: The site is located about 40 miles south and west of Green River on the McKinnon Road. Travel about 18 miles south on Wyoming Highway 530 to the Mckinnon Road junction and turn right. Proceed about 22 miles down this road to where the large power line crosses. Be aware of traffic since the only way to get to the high line service trail is by driving off of the shoulderless McKinnon Road. The McKinnon Road is elevated here and really should not be attempted by those who are unfamiliar with off-road travel. The ground is sandy and proper caution should be exercised. A more suitable parking situation could involve quite a long hike, which is preferable to waiting for a passing vehicle to pull you out or take you to a phone. It can get mighty lonely out here. The banded flint

Banded flint from near the powerlines just north of McKinnon.

starts at the edge of the McKinnon Road, though the bigger pieces seem more prevalent farther away from the road itself.

Rockhounding: The hardest part of this site is getting to it, though previous experience or living in this environment may make it easier.

At first the rocks all look rather drab as you bounce along the ruts. When the door swings open and your eyeballs stop vibrating, the dead come to life, in a manner of speaking. The otherwise dull rock takes on a whole new perspective when one can adequately focus.

There are well contrasted bands of brown and black that give an illusion of wood grain in a majority of these small to large pieces. Some have strongly contrasting grey to white inclusions billowing within and along their outer edges. These rocks are fairly brittle as indicated by the many broken pieces, and must have made a popular tool stone for Native Americans.

51   BROWN TURITELLA OF LITTLE AMERICA

Land type: Desert mesa.
Land manager: Bureau of Land Management.
Material: Fossils, jasper, agate, moss agate.
Tools: Rock hammer.
Vehicle: Utility.
Accommodations: Motels and restaurants at Little America within 10 miles.
Finding the site: The Westvaco exit (Exit 72) is located 16 miles west of Green River, or 3 miles east of Little America on Interstate 80. Go north at this exit to the frontage road and turn left to the FMC Road. Follow the FMC Road 2.2 miles to the Sweetwater County Road 57 and turn right. 1.3 miles farther up this road a narrow dirt road will take off to the right and climb up to the top of a flat ridge. Depending on conditions and the type of vehicle you are driving the last 1.3 miles just mentioned might best be made on foot.

Rockhounding: Agate and jasper of a variety of colors lay all over the top here. The wind-polished stones come in different sizes as well. A host of other treasures could exist within this deposit that only need the discerning eye of a persistent student.

Along the edges of the top are the turitella fossils. These are actually goniobasis fossils, but the turitella name seems to be permanently affixed. The majority of these are not agate quality, but they still offer a very adequate addition to any collection. With careful searching some agatized rock could be found.

While on top take time to note the large industrial plant. Should you decide to take advantage of the next site this information will be helpful.

Turitella and agate are found on top of the bluffs in the right- hand part of this picture.

51-52 *BROWN TURITELLA OF LITTLE AMERICA—ROCK QUARRY AGATE*

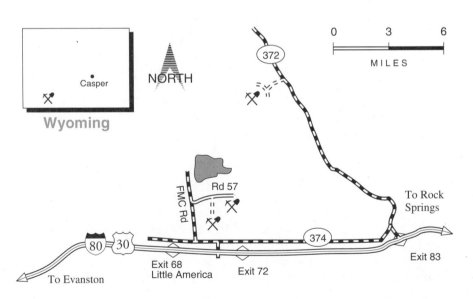

Land type: Badlands.
Land manager: Bureau of Land Management.
Material: Agate, fossils.
Tools: None.
Vehicle: Any.
Accommodations: Motels and restaurants at Little America within 30 miles.
Finding the site: Large weed-covered gravel piles are about 12 miles north of Interstate 80 on Wyoming Highway 372. Leave I-80 at Exit 83 and proceed north on WY 372 until you see the piles on your left or west side. There are several roads that lead over to the numerous piles so it is a matter of picking one and winding around toward the unseen edge of the ridge.

Rockhounding: Some walking will turn up agates just about anywhere in this obviously disturbed surface. Big ones, good for slabbing, come out of this kind of site because the heavy equipment of some past endeavor uncovered them—but finds are not as plentiful as at the previous site.

In the process of walking find some time to wander over to the edge and look south west. The large (FMC) plant that was north of site 51 now can be seen to the southwest. As you contemplate just how big this country is, drop over the edge a little and look around for some cliff-forming sandstone. When you find it, the familiar turitella (goniobasis) shell can be found. This will give you a very slight feel for the immensity of the deposit and a general idea of the geology. Armed with this information and personal experience, new discoveries are more of an educated survey as opposed to luck.

Agates are exposed in this old quarry with the FMC plant visible in the distance.

53 *FOSSIL FISH OF KEMMERER*

Land type: Badlands desert.
Land manager: Private, U.S. Government.
Material: Fossils.
Tools: None.
Vehicle: Any.
Accommodations: Restaurants and motels at Kemmerer within 10 miles.
Finding the site: Fossil Butte National Monument is located about 10 miles west of Kemmerer on U.S. Highway 30.

The 8,198-acre monument is administered and protected by the National Park Service. The visitor center is open year-round, providing an excellent source of information about the geologic history of the area.
Restrictions: Collecting of vertebrate fossils is prohibited on public lands, however collecting is allowed for a fee at the following quarries:

A. Ulrich's Fossil Quarries:
Highway 30 W
Fossil Station, WY 83101
(307) 877-6466
(307) 877-3289

It is not legal to collect specimens like these.

B. Warfield Springs Fossil Quarries
HCR 61 Box 301
Thayne, WY 83127
(307) 883-2445
C. Tynsky's Fossil Fish
476 Granite Dr.
Rock Springs, WY 82901
(307) 362-7557

Note: Public access to this quarry is not guaranteed. Specific details should be obtained by contacting the above address.
D. Tynsky's Fossils
201 Beryl St.
Kemmerer, WY 83101
(307) 877-6885

Note: Public access to this quarry is not guaranteed. Specific details should be obtained by contacting the above address.

Quarry sites:
A. Ulrich's Fossil Quarry
Tools: Provided.
Recommended items not provided: Sunglasses, gloves, drinking liquid, snacks, and layered clothing.
Finding Ulrich's Fossil Quarry: Transportation is provided to the quarry from Ulrich's Fossil Gallery, 10 miles west of Kemmerer on U.S. Highway 30.

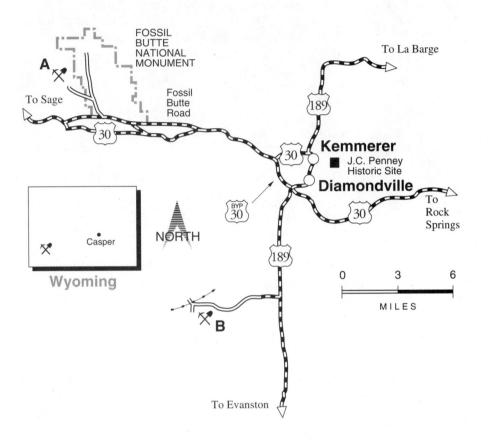

Rockhounding at Ulrich's Fossil Quarry: Quarrying does not begin until June 1 and closes on Labor Day. Advance reservations must be made; a staff member will be with you at all times.

The quarry operates seven days a week, weather permitting. Departure from the gallery at Fossil is at 9 a.m. (unless special arrangements are made) for approximately 3 hours. A reasonable amount of fossils can be retained from the recovery process, with the exception of those designated as "rare and unusual" by the State of Wyoming.

Children under ten have a special area provided to meet their individual needs. For more information on this opportunity contact the above address.

B. Warfield Springs Fossil Quarry
Accommodations: RV parking and tent sites but no hook ups. Restroom and shower available.

Finding the Warfield Springs Fossil Quarry: The quarry is reached from U.S. Highway 189 about 7 miles south of Kemmerer. If you are coming from Interstate 80 look for the sign about 6 miles north of the Bon Rico Club. This is also an entrance to a large sulphur shipping terminal, however there are signs directing you to the quarry 7 miles away.

If the road is wet and muddy do not try it without four wheel drive. When it is dry, the road should be no trouble.

Rockhounding at the Warfield Springs Fossil Quarry: The quarry is open from Memorial Day weekend until August 31. Reservations are not needed for groups of less than ten. When arriving at the quarry, you must stop in the parking area and register at the information center. There is an attendant at the quarry 7 days a week, 24 hours a day.

The fossils are recovered by prying large blocks of limestone loose and splitting them again and again using hammers and chisels. These tools and instructions for proper collecting techniques are included in the fee.

The collector can keep all but the rare specimens, which are retained by the quarry. Stingrays, turtles, birds, reptiles, and some fish over 18 inches are considered rare. Removing and restoring these rare fossils is very difficult and time consuming.

Children and pets are welcome, but someone must be free to watch them. Animals must be leashed and children supervised. The quarry cannot be responsible for their well-being. Children can collect fossils only if they are mature enough to handle the tools. If there is a member of your group who does not want to collect, they will not be charged. There is a shade porch and lots of space to hike around in.

Land type: Desert ridge.

Land manager: Bureau of Land Management, private.

Material: Turitella (goniobasis) agate, fossil, algae.

Tools: Optional, shovel, rock hammer.

Vehicle: Utility.

Accommodations: Motels and restaurants within 25 miles at Wamsutter.

Finding the site: Enter Wamsutter from Interstate 80 at Exit 173. Go south of the Interstate toward the Conoco station and

The black turitella from Wamsutter is a favorite among hounds.

turn left. At the yield sign make a right-hand turn on Sweetwater County Road 23. The county sign does not appear until after you cross the railroad tracks so don't sweat it right away. Follow this gravel road 8 miles to the Barrel Springs Road and turn right. Take this narrower road 10 miles to a metal shed (barn). At this junction there will be a sign with mileage and direction arrows. You will stay dead ahead on Windmill Draw Road, which is little more than two parallel ruts. The agate will be on the top of the rim about 1.5 miles farther.

The vast Red Desert stretches beyond camera capability for a fitting backdrop at the turitella beds of Wamsutter.

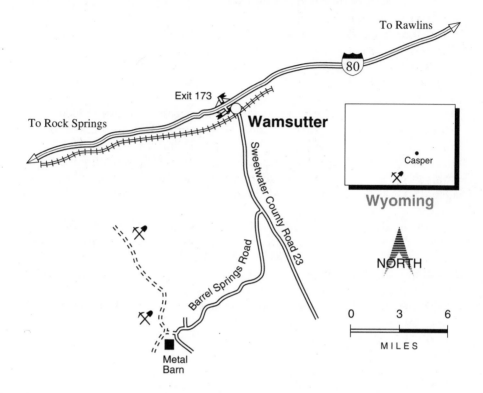

Rockhounding: Turitella is the common name among rockhounds for the fossil agate found here, although the proper name is goniobasis. If you talk to any local people remember to use the turitella name. It is not likely they will recognize the formal title. I am not even sure how to pronounce it.

Shells are virtually everywhere on the surface at this place. The better ones take some searching, with slabs the most prized. Some more enterprising hounds have dug for bigger pieces. Unless you have a very large amount of room with adequate shocks it is a process of selection. With careful cutting and polishing these specimens make extremely beautiful jewelry. The black color of these pieces is the most sought after as opposed to the brown or gray colored ones of different sites.

If you still have room, continue on up the road 2 miles and find a safe place to park. Fossil algae is on the surface here. This banded swirling material can come in different shades of brown. Again the process of selection is required for the better ones. Some of the pieces will take a good polish. There is an art to correctly slicing them, so grab enough to allow for experimentation.

Land type: Badlands.
Land manager: Bureau of Land Management, Wyoming State Land.
Materials: Fossils, agate, crystals.
Tools: Pointed object,(ice pick, customized screw driver, etc.) rock hammer and a carrying bag.
Vehicle: Any.
Accommodations: Motels and restaurants within 30 miles at Cody.
Finding the site: Go north of Cody on Wyoming Highway 120 about 29 miles. Turn right onto Wyoming Highway 294 and drive about 10 miles to a turnout just past Three Dam Road number 1210. The asphalt paved turnout is large enough to accommodate large semi trucks, though it is not designed to hold large numbers of them.

Rockhounding: Agates and calcite crystals can be found virtually anywhere. There are many sandstone beds on both sides of the road, though not all contain shells. The best shells so far have come from the south. They are easily damaged so care should be taken in removing them. The soft stone they are imbedded in easily separates and can be manipulated with a pointed object. Even a dull knife (or a sharp one, if you don't mind making it dull) can serve the purpose.

Shells and crystals are found in these outcrops along Wyoming Highway 294.

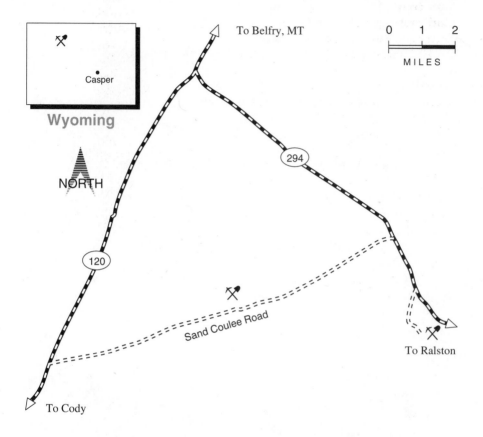

Gumbo makes up much of the landscape, so when rain does fall, or if you are the early spring type and snow still sets in the shadows, be prepared to get very muddy. DO NOT try an off-road excursion in your vehicle if the ground is wet. The rule of thumb I was taught about spring driving in this country is "If it ain't blacktop, it ain't road." This changes as the warm summer wind dries things to a hard crust, but all that looks dry in the aftermath of a spring rain shower is not.

Going back toward Cody, the Sand Coulee Road will make an interesting side trip. It is not the best road and many ruts will outline just how entertaining it can be. As you drive toward Cody, badland hills color the horizon to the west. Small rises between the badlands and the roadway have some calcite crystals formed in the crevices. These crystals are more of a yellow color than the clear variety found at the shell site. They do take some searching and for the most part are the only noticeable stone worth picking up.

Land type: Mountainous.

Land manager: Shoshone National Forest

Material: Volcanic rocks, banded gneiss.

Tools: None, (unless you prefer to make smaller chunks out of the bigger ones).

Vehicle: Any.

Accommodations: Motels and restaurants within 25 miles at Cooke City, Montana.

Finding the site: The road cuts are about 2 miles west of the Chief Joseph Highway/ Wyoming Highway 120 on U.S. Highway 212. There are adequate places to pull off on paved areas to be out of traffic.

Rockhounding: The banded volcanic rocks here are very obvious. There are loose ones laying in the borrow ditch, so chipping them out of the hard cliff structure—which is illegal— is not required. Plenty of larger boulders are already separated from the wall, so there is no need to risk a fine and increase erosion problems.

Be sure to bring plenty of film. The mountain scenery will provide many excellent photo opportunities.

Road cuts along U.S. Highway 212 offer photographic options with some amazing rock samples.

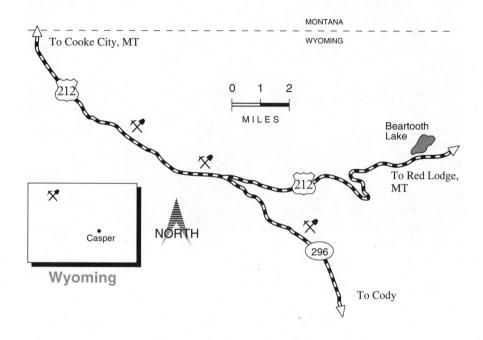

57 SUNLIGHT BASIN AGATES

Land type: Mountain valley.
Land manager: Shoshone National Forest.
Material: Agate (chalcedony), petrified wood, gold.
Tools: Gold pan, shovel.
Vehicle: Any.
Accommodations: Motels and restaurants within 30 miles.
Finding the site: Coming out of Yellowstone National Park on U.S. Highway 212 proceed through Cooke City to Wyoming Highway 296 (otherwise known as the Chief Joseph Highway). Turn to your right and travel about 26 miles to the Sunlight Basin Road. Just before the turnoff you will cross a unique bridge spanning an extremely deep canyon. There is a parking area on the opposite side for those that want to investigate more. The well marked Sunlight Basin Road is just past this bridge on WY 296.

Coming out of Cody on Wyoming Highway 120 drive about 17 miles to the Chief Joseph Highway turnoff. It is well marked. Turn to the left on this paved road and go about 13 miles over Dead Indian Pass. It is quite

Sunlight Creek river gravels offer new treasures every year.

a breathtaking view, making a camera essential. At the bottom of the pass you will cross Dead Indian Creek with a campground to your right. Keep going on around the "hill" and down another not-so-steep grade to the Sunlight Basin Road.

Turn onto the gravel road and stay alert for wildlife. There are 12 miles of scenic road to the camping area with many opportunities to see deer, elk, coyote, and other wild residents. Little Sunlight Campground is in grizzly country. You can stop at the ranger station about 8 miles in for current bear information, rules, and safety precautions.

Rockhounding: The river gravels provide the easiest but also the most frustrating hunting. When the level of water is down during the late summer there is new material revealed from the spring flooding. The specimens are somewhat worn for the wear but worthwhile, not to mention the added benefit of beautiful scenery. Just beyond the campground along the road cuts there are some promising prospects, though it may take a more careful search.

For the more industrious the stream beds could produce some elusive gold. It does not jump into the pan. Hard work and calculated effort is required to separate this precious metal from its concealing earth garments.

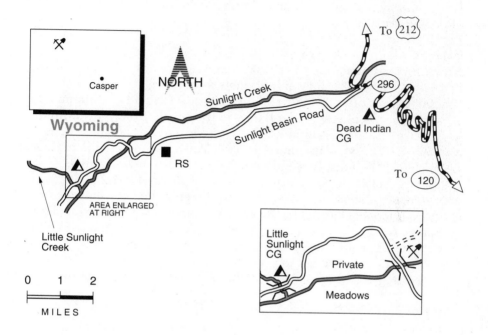

Casper

NORTH

Wyoming

Sunlight Creek

Sunlight Basin Road

To 212

296

Dead Indian
CG

To 120

RS

AREA ENLARGED
AT RIGHT

Little Sunlight
Creek

Little
Sunlight
CG

Private

Meadows

0   1   2

M I L E S

Land type: Badlands.
Land manager: Bureau of Land Management.
Material: Fossils.
Tools: None.
Vehicle: Any.
Accommodations: Since the site is almost within the city limits of Cody, a variety of stores, restaurants, and motels are nearby.
Special attractions: The Buffalo Bill Historical Center is within minutes of the site, and could take several days to fully explore on its own. Among the attractions are the Whitney Gallery of Western Art, and the Plains Indian and Winchester museums. Old Trail Town is also near the museum site with Old West displays and artifacts well worth investigation.
Finding the site: In Cody turn off of U.S. Highway 14/16/20 onto Stampede Avenue. A stop light is located at this intersection, which helps identify it. Follow Stampede Avenue west and continue following Skyline Drive as Stampede Avenue terminates. A golf course will be on the left before crossing an irrigation ditch and then a cattle guard, which is about 1 mile from "red lake." The red dirt to your left is usually dry, though when it does rain a lot there are some puddles. Find a safe place to park off of the road.

The fossils are found "in the lake" between this hound and the access road seen in the middle of the photograph.

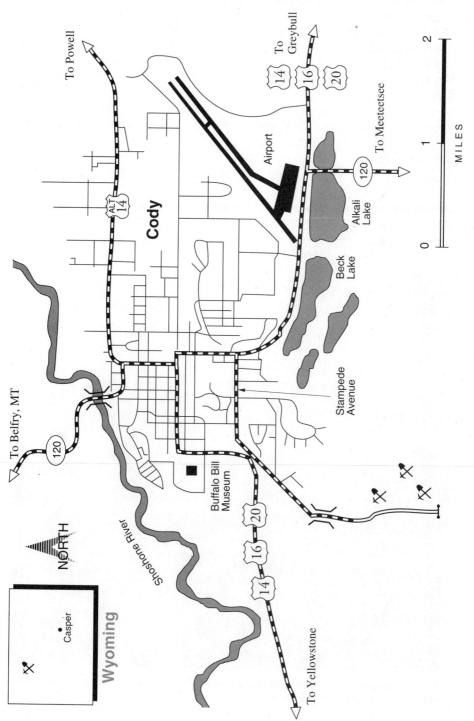

To Powell

To Greybull

To Meeteetse

14 16 20

Airport

Cody

ALT 14

Alkali Lake

Beck Lake

Stampede Avenue

MILES

0 1 2

To Belfry, MT

120

120

NORTH

Shoshone River

Wyoming

Casper

Buffalo Bill Museum

20

16

14

To Yellowstone

Rockhounding: Be aware of the high use of this area by ATV riders. Most are not aware of the fossils and are much more interested in improving their high-speed off-road skills. Conflicts are rare, but it is good to be aware of other users and expect the unexpected.

Belemnites and other shell fossils can be rescued from further abuse all along the "lake bottom." The shells that remain are not as large as earlier finds, but they still offer a pleasant addition to any collection. The hills to the east of the area are also appealing, though it is as yet undetermined exactly what they may offer.

An active gypsum quarry that supplies the Celotex plant north of Cody is at the end of this road. No public access is allowed, and during the week haul trucks use this road to transport ore to the plant. Be sure to park appropriately.

59   PETRIFIED WOOD OF THE NORTH FORK

Land type: Mountainous river bottom.
Land manager: Bureau of Land Management.
Material: Petrified wood.
Tools: None.
Vehicle: Any.

High waters create a new display every year, though it's not accessible during this purging.

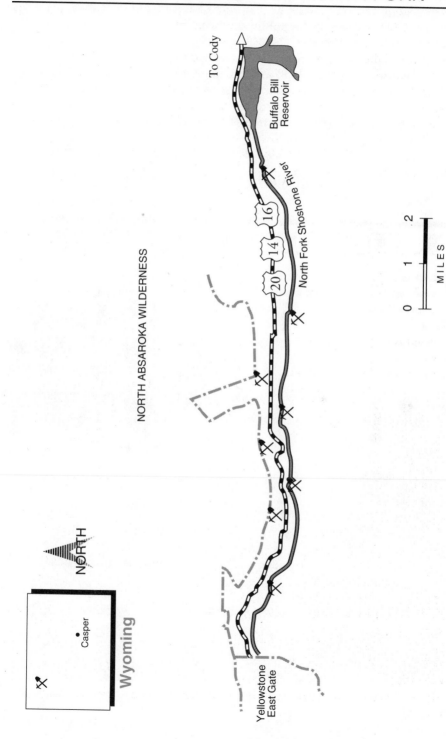

Accommodations: Restaurants and motels at Cody within 15 miles.
Finding the site: Go west of Cody on U.S. Highway 14/16/20, past the Buffalo Bill Reservoir. Turn left on Park County Road 6KV about 13 miles from Cody. Proceed to the public access area for the river.

Rockhounding: Spring runoff is not a good time to consider looking here, so if you are an early arrival, another site would be a better choice.

The river is continuously turning up new stones. Agatized wood is constantly being uncovered and rolled downstream, so the search here is a matter of timing and persistence. The whole stream bed is a potential hunting site, though access is difficult in places.

Because the river brings new discoveries year after year, return visits are especially appealing

60 PETRIFIED WOOD OF THE SOUTH FORK

Land type: Mountain stream.
Land manager: Shoshone National Forest.
Material: Agatized wood.
Tools: None.
Vehicle: Any.
Accommodations: Restaurants and motels at Cody within 30 miles.
Finding the site: On your way through Cody on U.S. Highway 14/16/20 look for and turn left on Wyoming Highway 291. Travel down this road about 30 miles. The blacktop will end before you reach the National Forest, so

A variety of colors is presented in the agatized wood found on the South Fork Shoshone.

don't panic, even though it seems like a very long trip. When the 30-mile indicator rolls across your odometer look closely for small signs indicating public access to the river.

Rockhounding: Here, as at the previous site, the water level needs to be low enough to reveal the gravel beds. The colorful agatized pieces of wood are easy to spot, but seem to be a long ways apart. One might consider a little fishing for a break between searches.

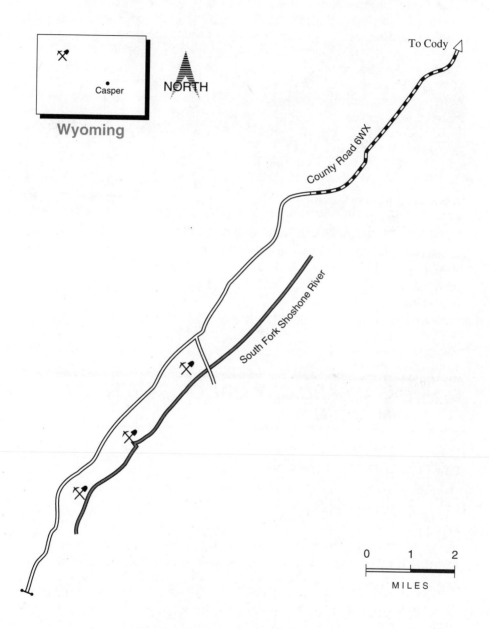

To Cody

County Road 6WX

South Fork Shoshone River

NORTH

Casper

Wyoming

0   1   2
MILES

Cameras and fishing gear could be included for the wood hunt on the South Fork Shoshone River.

61 BASALT AND CRYSTAL OF CARTER MOUNTAIN

Land type: Mountain.
Land manager: Shoshone
National Forest.
Material: Basalt, crystals and other related volcanic rocks.
Tools: Rock hammer (optional).
Vehicle: Any.
Accommodations: Restaurants and motels at Cody within 30 miles.
Finding the site: On your way to the Southfork Shoshone River of the previous site take note of the Castle Rock historical marker. This marker is 16 miles from Cody on Wyoming Highway 291. The Carter Mountain/National Forest Access Road is 2 miles past this historical marker. If you are more interested in high mountain scenery and would rather take a few pictures before adding to your growing pile of treasures, turn left on this gravel road. Follow the road for 12 miles to a long beautiful meadow at the base of a multicolored mountain.

A mountain of crystals and other specialities is steadily weathered out for those who can let go of the camera and look.

Rockhounding: The better rocks come from the many washes directly off the mountain. Be careful as the upper parts could break loose at any time.

The basalt is in either red or black color and almost looks like pumice, though it is heavier. The primary attraction is the exposed cavities of crystal. As various rocks tumble down the steep slopes they are broken open to reveal some well-formed specimens. A rock hammer could open up new treasures, though there are more than enough to fill a sack.

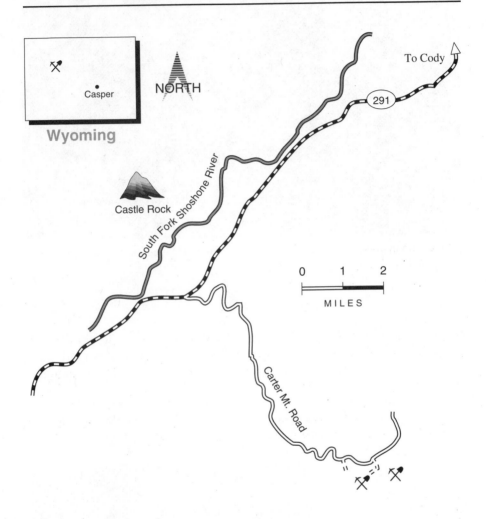

Wyoming
Casper
NORTH
To Cody
291
Castle Rock
South Fork Shoshone River
Carter Mt. Road

0   1   2
MILES

62 COLORED CHALCEDONY ALONG HIGHWAY 120

Land type: Badlands.
Land manager: Bureau of Land Management.
Material: Chalcedony, fossils
Tools: None.
Vehicle: Utility.
Accommodations: Restaurants and motels at Cody within 8 miles.
Finding the site: Take Wyoming Highway 120 south of Cody and watch for the landfill turnout, 3.2 miles away. Set your odometer here and at 1 mile, turn off of the highway across a cattle guard onto a rough dirt road. If it's wet, do not try it. Travel this road for the next 1.2 miles to the white formations you can see below the horizon.

Rockhounding: The "bubble" formations here come in different shades of red or blue. They are unique in their own fashion and can be very nice additions to a living room display. The bigger ones are exposed along the crests of the white formation mentioned as a landmark to guide you.

After filling up with all the samples your car dare hold take note of the sandstone formations on the way out. With a little searching one can find some well-preserved shell fossils along these exposures. These are encased in some rather soft rock and are hard to keep preserved, so appropriate measures should be taken.

These parallel ruts lead to the white-colored gumbo with some beautiful orange chalcedony.

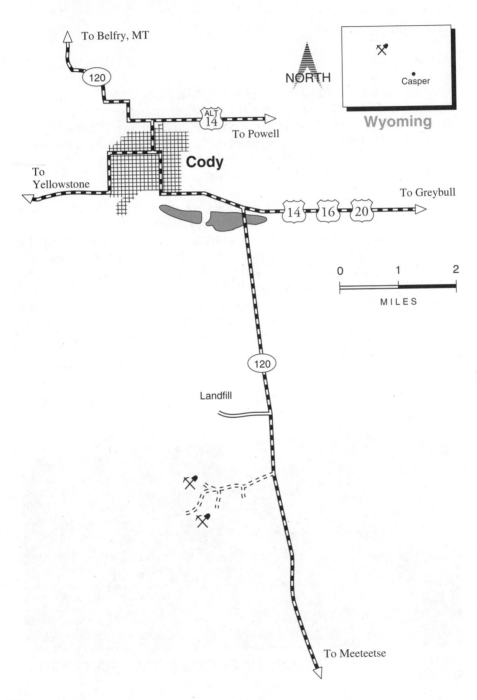

To Belfry, MT

120

NORTH

Wyoming

Casper

ALT 14

To Powell

To Yellowstone

Cody

To Greybull

14 — 16 — 20

0   1   2

MILES

120

Landfill

To Meeteetse

Land type: Mountain.
Land manager: National Forest.
Material: Copper minerals, gold.
Tools: Rock hammer (optional), gold pan and shovel.
Vehicle: A four-wheel drive is needed if you intend to drive to the ghost town itself; otherwise any vehicle can make it to the campground.
Accommodations: Motels and restaurants at Meeteetse within 20 miles.
Special attractions: Kirwin Ghost Town.
Finding the site: Meeteetse is on Wyoming Highway 120 about 31 miles southeast of Cody. At Meeteetse turn to the southwest onto Wyoming Highway 290. About 6 miles up this road turn to the left on Wood River Road. There is a sign just before the turnoff and the asphalt road is across the river, so don't panic when you go past a small dirt trail with an even smaller Wood River sign pointing to the left. The road you want is well marked with a big sign and plenty of room to accommodate two lanes of traffic.

For about the next 12 miles the road gradually changes to a much narrower and rougher dirt path. The last campground is called Brown Mountain. The 9 miles past the campground leads to the Kirwin ghost town. Four wheel drive is definitely recommended for these 9 miles.

Rockhounding: The river gravels offer the best selection of material. It takes a little walking to initially find the color most desired. However, it seems that when one beautiful piece is discovered there are more very close by. With a little searching a blue or green streak will share seams of white quartz sandwiched in an otherwise plain looking rock.

If you choose not to grind your way the additional 9 miles up to the ghost town there are plenty of enticing things to explore near the campground. For those with energy and a craving for gold the creek bed could be very rewarding.

The Kirwin ghost town area is off limits to collecting, but a journey into this remote part of Wyoming is an adventure all its own. The "road," if this trail can be called such, is an experience all in itself. A fair part of the track is the actual creek bed, complete with an active, water-up-to-the-doors creek. One spot requires driving up the stream for at least 50 feet. There are signs that the route and the creek have been moved more than once by periodic floods. Early in the year it might not be possible to reach the ghost town by vehicle. The first seekers will no doubt need to exercise their trailblazing skills.

Take plenty of film, and if you hike late in the day pack some warm clothing. When the sun goes over the mountain, so does the heat. There was some exploration work done in the area not long ago. The modern buildings are easy to spot, but there were plenty of old buildings still left at the time of this writing for spectacular pictures.

One of the Old West mine shafts at the Kirwin ghost town.

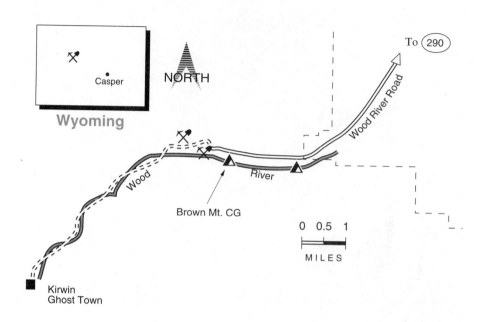

64   *GYPSUM AND CALCITE SOUTH OF LOVELL*

Land type: Badlands.

Land manager: Bureau of Land Management.

Material: Gypsum and calcite crystals, fossils, jasper, agate.

Tools: None.

Vehicle: Utility.

Accommodations: Restaurants and motels at Lovell within 15 miles.

Finding the site: Lovell is 46 miles east of Cody on U.S. Highway Alternate 14. Take U.S. Highway 310/Wyoming Highway 789 on the east side of Lovell for about 7 miles

Agates are also available in the Jasper field, though some close inspection may be required for any big ones.

south. Look for the sign directing you to the Georgia Pacific plant on your

Belemnites are found sharing the surface here, not far from the gypsum crystals.

left. Turn left on this blacktop road and continue for about 6 miles to the Spence Oil Field road. Turn right on this improved dirt road and look for a safe area to park. From here to the next right-hand turn about 1.5 miles away is Site A.

Your next decision will be whether to go right or left at the previously mentioned intersection. If you go left there will be some oil tanks and derricks to your left about 3 miles out. Go past them another mile to a fork in the road and stay to the right or park somewhere out of the way. The bridge will be plain to see along with the visible crystal beds. This is Site B.

If you decide to go to the right follow this rougher dirt road for about 2 miles to the badland hills easily distinguishable in the distance. This is Site C.

Rockhounding: At Site A, you will be driving through the middle of a fossil bed. On either side of the gravel road all the way to the right-hand turn leading to another site there are shells, belemnites, and selenite crystals. These are easy to spot laying on top of the ground virtually everywhere.

The "gyp-bed" formation at Site B is dominant in the whole region. My family found special pleasure in exploring the gray cliff exposure along the creek bank. The crystals are layered within the bank, and eroded pieces litter the ground. These soft crystals are very fragile. Proper arrangements should be made for their transport.

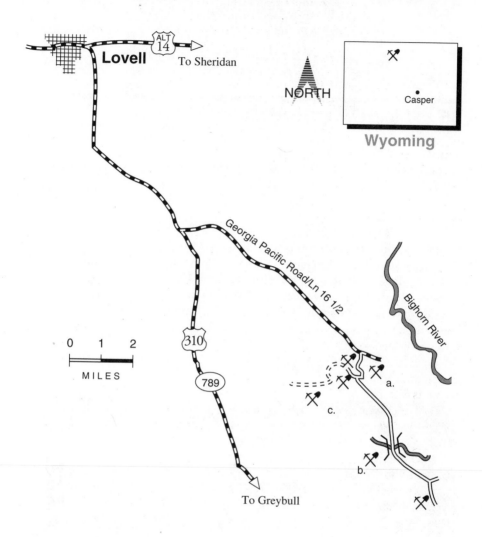

Extra care should be taken along the cliff side itself. The host rock is unstable at best. Some of the chunks that have fallen are large enough to cause serious injury.

At Site C, look for contrasting bands of color within walking distance of the two parallel ruts you are driving in and find a safe place to park. There is not much traffic, but the route is used, so don't block it. A person always thinks about being back in a few seconds only to find that the short walk turned into an afternoon marathon.

As a general rule—but by no means an absolute one—jasper is found in a nodule form washing out of the gray to whitish popcorn gumbo. None of those terms probably mean anything to a science major but that is how I describe it to my 12-year-old and he seems to understand. The washes can produce very fine pieces as well, though it is, for the most part, badly fractured.

65   BIGHORN AGATE

Land type: Mountains.
Land manager: Bighorn National Forest.
Material: Agate, crystals, conglomerate.
Tools: Rock hammer, chisel.
Vehicle: Utility.
Accommodations: Camping and mountain lodge within 12 miles. Additional restaurants and motels at Tensleep within 35 miles.
Finding the site: Deerhaven Lodge is on U.S. Highway 16, about 15 miles east of Tensleep. If you are traveling west on US 16 from Buffalo, the lodge will be about 3 miles west of the Meadowlark Resort. Turn onto Forest Road 27, which is also the entrance to the Deerhaven Lodge and proceed past the campground continuing north. Turn left onto Forest Road 24, 1

Interesting conglomerate samples are abundant in the Soldier Creek area.

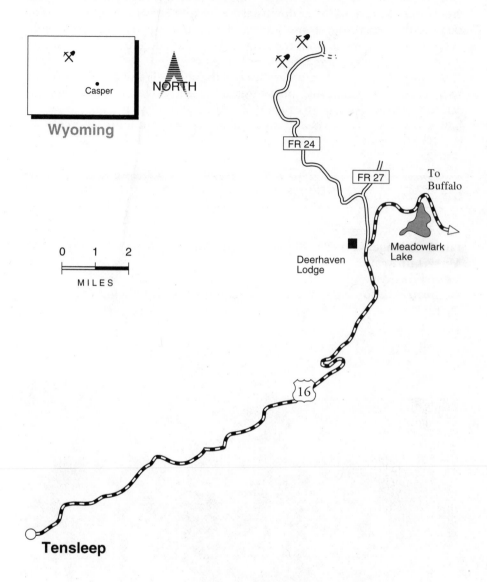

Wyoming
Casper
NORTH

0 1 2
MILES

FR 24
FR 27
To Buffalo
Deerhaven Lodge
Meadowlark Lake

16

Tensleep

mile after leaving the blacktop at US 16. Stay on Forest Road 24 to Soldier Creek, about 8 miles down this now dirt road. A sign pointing to the side will announce the Soldier Creek Cow Camp to aid your search.

Rockhounding: Bands of agate are locked up within various sizes of larger stone here. Some of the larger pieces will require some extensive hammer and chisel work to free the agate. Smaller pieces can be found along the creek and road bed already downsized either by heavy equipment or erosion. With an adventuresome spirit and lots of energy a hound could coax even better specimens from the neighboring cliffs and hillsides could produce even better specimens.

A unique type of conglomerate rock is found all along the creek and bank-side hills. These are most interesting and have prompted many a question from visitors when spotted in our yard display. They may not have the value, nor the beauty of a polished stone, but these strange color combinations attract every eye.

66 SPANISH POINT AGATE

Land type: Mountain.
Land manager: Private, Bureau of Land Management.
Material: Agate.
Vehicle: Any.
Accommodations: Restaurants and motels at Greybull within 15 miles of Shell.

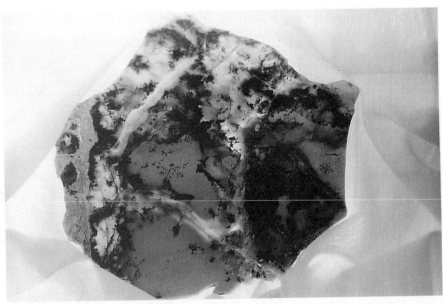

The sought after Spanish Point Agate is once again available with proper permission.

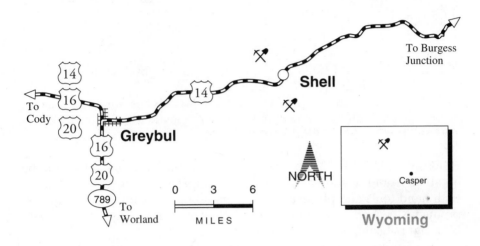

Finding the site: Arrangements for rockhounding in this fee area must be made by contacting Tom Garland, Shell Gem and Rock Shop; Box 136, Shell Route; Greybull; WY; 82426; (307) 765-2841.

Rockhounding: The Spanish Point Agate is well known and sought after. The mine itself is some distance out of Shell on private land; BLM hold the mineral rights. It is a seasonal area and the mountain weather can change unexpectedly. With advance arrangements, and an ear for weather conditions, this could be a very productive trip.

67   TRAPPER CREEK: AGATE MINE

Land type: Mountain.
Land manager: Private.
Material: Agate.
Tools: None.
Vehicle: Any.

> See Map on page 135

Accommodations: Restaurants and motels at Greybull within 40 miles.
Special attractions: The Greybull museum.
Finding the site: The Trapper Creek Agate Mine is best found by making arrangements with the mine owner. Contact Floyd "Kit" Smith, P.O. Box 145, Shell, WY. 82441. Phone (307) 765-2971.

Rockhounding: This is a fee area site and further information should be obtained from the address above. The Trapper Creek agate is recovered with hand tools and physical labor from an open pit mine. The finished product is well appreciated by the beholders, though it does require slabbing and polishing for the best effect.

   To get an idea of what the agate looks like in the rough and to browse through other wonders, stop at the Greybull Museum. An ammonite 5 feet in diameter resides there with other worthwhile educational displays.

68   FOSSILS AT MEDICINE MOUNTAIN

Land type: Badland desert bordering rough mountainous terrain.
Land manager: Bureau of Land Management.
Material: Fossils, chalcedony, crystals.
Tools: Rock hammer, chisel, bag.
Vehicle: Utility.
Accommodations: Motels and restaurants at Lovell within 20 miles, camping.
Special attractions: Bighorn Canyon National Recreation Area.
Finding the site: Lovell is 46 miles east of Cody on U.S. Highway Alternate 14. Continue east of Lovell on US 14A toward Burgess Junction for about 10 miles. A long, flat, straight piece of the highway will obviously cross the southern end of Bighorn Lake. After crossing this stretch to the east side of the lake make a left-hand turn and proceed north on the gravel road for about 3.5 miles. On a clear day—which most of them are—you will see a narrow road climbing up the red mountainside in the distance. It is just below that cut that you will want to end up. Follow the main road, which is identified by its width and (rapidly disappearing) maintenance. As

Fossil shell conglomerate from the limestone of Medicine Mountain.

you enter a narrow canyon where the road starts climbing steeply, stay to the right a very short distance to an old quarry.

Rockhounding: The red ridges directly to the right of the parking area contain some very promising chalcedony pieces. The drusy quartz appearance enhances the attractive specimens that are laying in the washes in a variety of sizes. Most of them are reddish, with some bluish gray. Some even have a spotted red inclusion that is very interesting indeed.

Shell fossils are found in the limestone cliffs along the steep draw to the left. It is a large cliff; in fact there are several. The fossils take a bit of a search, but when they are found the abundance is staggering. These take some selective hammering and careful chiseling, unlike the chalcedony. In and among the scattered rocks you will find crystals in the crevices. These are not always easy to remove due to the placement and hardness of the host rock. There is no shortage of smaller samples, however.

FOSSILS AT MEDICINE MOUNTAIN—
FIVE SPRINGS FOSSILS

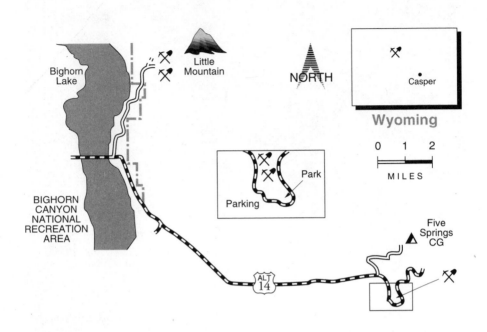

---

69   *FIVE SPRINGS FOSSILS*

Land type: Badland desert mountainside.

Land manager: Bureau of Land Management.

Material: Belemnites, oyster shell, dahlite nodules.

Tools: Bag.

Vehicle: Any.

Accommodations: Five Springs Campground is a small but pleasant camp. There is a waterfall within walking distance for those with enough energy to tackle the mountain-

Dahlite nodules found in the greenish shale along U.S. Highway Alternate 14.

Belemnites and dahlite nodules are found above the road here.

ous trail. The narrow steep road is not the best. Vehicles over 30 feet long are advised not to venture the 2 miles to the campground. Motels and restaurants at Lovell within 25 miles.

Finding the site: Lovell is 46 miles east of Cody on U.S. Highway Alternate 14. Go east of Lovell about 20 miles on US 14A. Continue about 0.5 miles past the Five Springs Campground. As of this writing there is a pull-out area on the right side near some black to gray shale. Also, as the highway makes a hairpin turn another 0.5 mile past this pullout area, a wide flat area is currently being used as a storage place for gravels and road construction equipment.

At any parking spot there will be some hiking involved. Since this is the bottom part of a very steep grade be especially careful of any traffic—they may not be able to stop, or could need all the speed they can muster to make the grade.

Rockhounding: Between the red of the mountainside and the black of the pillowy ridges melting into the desert. Look for a green shale full of fossils. The belemnites are the most prevalent and show age and weather. Shells are mixed with belemnites on the surface here.

In the upper regions of the black-to-gray shale bordering the green fossil beds are dahlite nodules. These rascals are hard to spot until you finally do pinpoint one. After that they seem to sprout like weeds. In fact, a number of them are only partially revealed and are often in the shadow of some plant. When split they show a very unique structure with some crystal formations in a few of the specimens.

Selenite crystals can be found in the black shale on the opposite side of the highway. These crystals show a dirty brown stain, however, and may not be desirable.

70 CRYSTAL CREEK FOSSILS

Land type: Badlands.
Land manager: Bureau of Land Management.
Material: Belemnites, shells, chalcedony.
Tools: Rock hammer, bag.
Vehicle: Any, however conditions could make a utility much more useful.
Accommodations: Motels and restaurants at Lovell within 20 miles.
Finding the site: Lovell is 46 miles east of Cody on U.S. Highway Alternate 14. At Lovell travel east on US 14A past Bighorn Lake. Crystal Creek Road is well marked on the right-hand side about 3 miles past Bighorn Lake. Site A is about 6 miles down this gravel road in the badlands. It is a wide road here with relatively safe parking along the edge. There is traffic, though, so be careful and considerate. Site B is about 4 miles past Site A. After crossing some flat, private ground turn left at the intersection and

Site C of the Crystal Creek site has an abundance of belemnites.

go about 0.5 mile into the badlands again. Site C is found by following this gravel road around the butte for about 3 miles to where the roads meet again. Take a left here and go about 1 mile to the Crystal Creek Road sign and turn right on the now dirt road. Follow this road along the mountainside for about 1.5 miles to the green shale.

Rockhounding: Site A nestles within a long draw intercepted by the road. Some colorful chalcedony similar to Dryhead agate pops up here and there. (Dryhead agate comes from north of here in Montana. Sites for this beauty are discussed in *Rockhounding Montana*.) The green shale here contains a multitude of belemnites and shells between the limestone cliffs and the white gypsum.

Site B holds belemnites and shells on both sides of the road. A butte on the right side gently slopes away for a great distance with the road passing through the fossil bed. The better shells seem be closer to the butte. Bigger and more complete belemnites come from the opposite side of the road, away from the gullies.

Site C presents more fossils and chalcedony. The chalcedony here is blue as opposed to the red of Site A. In addition to the belemnites and shells, the top of the limestone ridges produced a "fossil hash." This conglomerate of pieces of shell, scales, or whatever is an interesting specimen in a class all its own. A rock hammer might be useful in separating the better pieces. The green shale here is predominantly on the left of the road, though one could probably identify quite a bit of the deposit all along here.

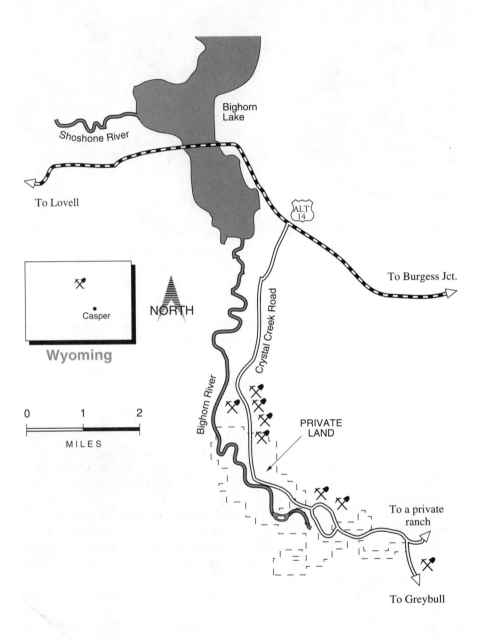

Bighorn
Lake

Shoshone River

To Lovell

ALT
14

To Burgess Jct.

Wyoming

Casper

NORTH

Crystal Creek Road

Bighorn River

PRIVATE
LAND

To a private
ranch

0   1   2

MILES

To Greybull

Land type: Desert hills.
Land manager: Wyoming State Department of Transportation.
Material: Chert, iron pyrite crystals, shell fossils.
Tools: Hammer and chisel are helpful but not required.
Vehicle: Any.
Accommodations: Motels and restaurants at Shoshoni within 11 miles.

Samples of banded chert from the Birdseye site.

Finding the site: Shoshoni is about 25 miles east of Riverton on U.S. Highway 26/Wyoming Highway 789. Drive north of Shoshoni on U.S. Highway 20/WY 789 for 8.6 miles to the Birdseye Road. Turn to the right onto this gravel road and travel 2.7 miles to the former quarry on the left side.

Rockhounding: The limestone cliffs contain seams of gray banded chert of various thickness. The seams are plainly visible, but there are plenty of

Looking down on the old quarry from the limestone cliffs with imbedded chert.

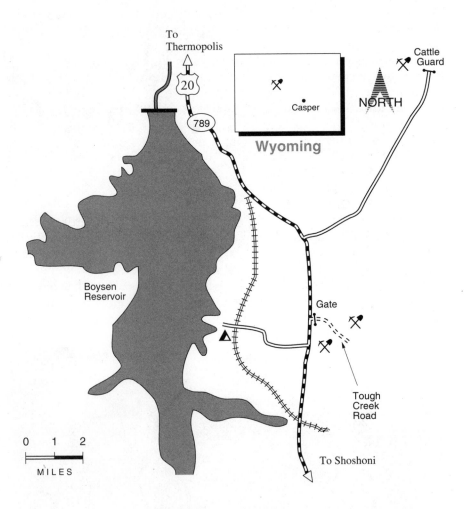

loose samples to choose from.

On your way to the higher cliffs note the loose rock. There are an abundance of small iron pyrite crystals in various locations. Some of these crystals are combined with and included as part of fossil sea shells. Some of the boulders are large and will require chiseling to separate the keepers.

Land type: Desert prairie.
Land manager: Wyoming State Land, Bureau
of Land Management, private.
Material: Petrified wood, agate, quartz, mica schist, and others yet to be
discovered.
Tools: None.
Vehicle: Any. (This dirt road is virtually impassable when wet.)
Accommodations: Shoshoni motels and restaurants within 6 miles. Various campgrounds along Boysen Reservoir.
Finding the site: Shoshoni is about 25 miles east of Riverton on U.S. Highway 26/Wyoming Highway 789. Drive north of Shoshoni on US 20/WY 789
for 6 miles to the Tough Creek Road sign. Turn to the right onto this dirt
road and park safely inside the fence. There is a barbed wire gate that will
require opening and closing. The wire can cut so be careful.

Rockhounding: The wind polished material is laying on the surface all
over here. This makes it easy to spot, and hard to pick which specimens
to leave. The sizes range from fingernail to two-handed pieces. A rock
hammer is useful in prying some of the bigger ones loose. There are plenty
of smaller ones to fill your sack without the big ones.

There are more pretty rocks than ugly ones piled up at Tough Creek.

Land type: Mountainous desert
Land manager: BLM, private.
Material: Feldspar, quartz, beryl, garnets.
Tools: Rock hammer.
Vehicle: Utility.
Accommodations: Motels and cafes at Shoshoni within 20 miles.
Finding the site: Shoshoni is about 25 miles east of Riverton on U.S. Highway 26/Wyoming Highway 789. About 3 miles north of Shoshoni on US 20/WY 789 turn to the east onto Bonneville Road. Travel 4 miles down this asphalt road to Badwater Road. The asphalt turns to dirt as you turn left here. Follow Badwater Road to the next left turn onto the Quien Sabe Road, 3 miles away. Take this dirt road 5 miles north to a narrow draw where the road splits. The wider better one bearing dead ahead usually has a padlocked gate on it. Turn to the right here and proceed 2 miles to a private residence. At the cattle guard there is a trail veering to the right. Follow this trail to the top of the ridge about 1.5 miles farther.

Rockhounding: Private land is a real concern so be extra attentive of signs and fences. If in doubt, ask. The draws and washes you cross just after turning to the right off of Quien Sabe road have some real nice green feld-

Some interesting rocks come from the Shoshoni Aquamarine site.

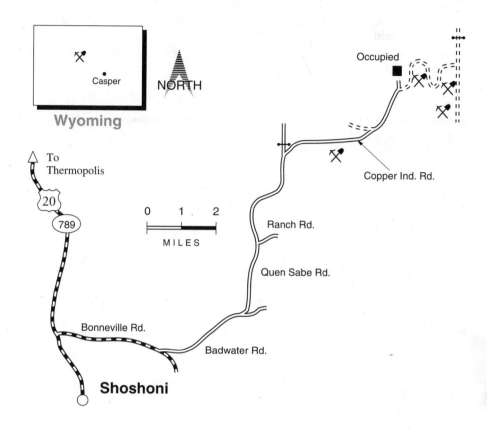

Wyoming

Casper

NORTH

To Thermopolis

20

789

0 1 2
MILES

Occupied

Copper Ind. Rd.

Ranch Rd.

Quen Sabe Rd.

Bonneville Rd.

Badwater Rd.

Shoshoni

spar samples. There is also an abundance of quartz, the greater part being of the white variety. With some searching there are other colors of the hard wind-polished quartz showing some real promise. Some are reminiscent of rose quartz, though not near the quality of the Black Hills specimens.

When you arrive at the private home there is an obvious fence and a cattle guard. The trail to the right is a little hard to see at first, but changes quickly to a well-defined route. If you are not in a hurry you might visit with the owner of the house. When a person lives this far out of town they generally appreciate knowing what you are there for—and they may know of a new hot spot.

After arriving on the top of the ridge find a safe place to park and proceed to search. Toward the southern end there is a report of garnets, though I have not yet found any. All the same, there are plenty of other specimens to study while hoping for the big strike.

Beryl has been mined in this area for a long time, though there is no active mining now. There are reports of aquamarine, which is associated with beryl, in the pegmatites of the area , but the places to look for the crystal are on private ground and would involve some patient research. The resistance I found in that pursuit caused me to look for other treasures in different places. All the same, the green feldspar is a type of microcline which could prove to be a worthwhile lapidary stone—a consideration that could make the trip worthwhile.

74 WIND RIVER IRIS AGATE

Land type: River bottom.
Land manager: Bureau of Land Management, private, Wind River Indian Reservation.
Material: Agate, petrified wood.
Tools: Rock hammer.
Vehicle: Any.
Accommodations: Restaurants and motels at Riverton or Dubois depending on distance.
Finding the site: The Wind River runs through Dubois past Riverton to the Boysen Reservoir.

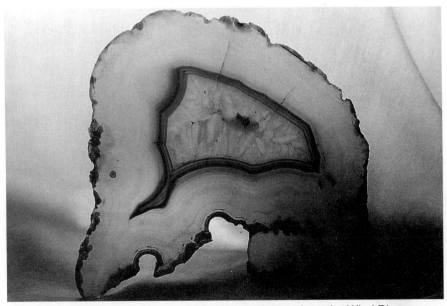

The elusive "iris" agate can be found by the persistent along the Wind River.

Rockhounding: The gravels of the Wind River produce what is called the Wind River Iris Agate. This particular agate will reflect the light of the rainbow in sunlight when sliced thinly. The limb casts are more often found near Riverton, though access to the river here is not the easiest. As a general rule tribal lands are closed to rockhounding. There is a rock quarry in Riverton that offers some real potential, but again, access is not guaranteed. The public access areas outside the Reservation are closer to Dubois and the easiest to reach. Obviously these places are not the closest to Riverton, which reduces their productivity.

74 WIND RIVER IRIS AGATE

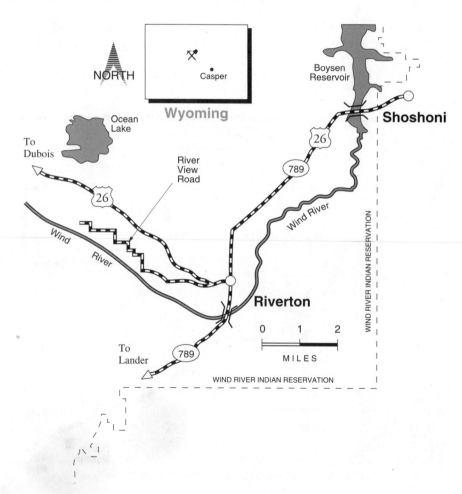

Land type: Mountains.
Best season: Late summer.
Land manager: Shoshone National Forest.
Material: Agate, petrified wood, fossils, quartz.
Tools: Rock hammer (optional).
Vehicle: Utility, four wheel drive recommended.
Accommodations: Motels and restaurants at Dubois within 20 miles.
Special attraction: Tie Hack Memorial.
Finding the sites: The Tie Hack Memorial is 16.4 miles west of Dubois on U.S. Highway 26/287. Turn onto Long Creek Road, (Forest Road 513), 0.7 mile past the memorial. Travel 1.7 miles to Forest Road 548 and determine if the "Not recommended for use" sign applies to you. The second site is over the ridge 3 miles farther. Turn off on the unmarked road near the bottom. This can be very treacherous and should be avoided when muddy.

Rockhounding: The first site produced smaller pieces of petrified wood. They are not the prized type found from the Wiggin's formation, though

75 THOROFARE AGATE

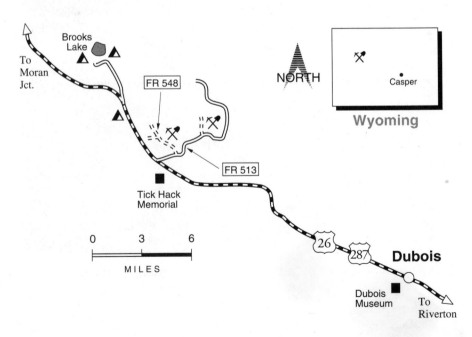

Creek beds and washouts along Long Creek produce agates and fossils.

there could be some washed out at some point. The specimens are easiest to find in the washes and exposed road cuts; it can be somewhat of a walk to each one.

The second site produced a limb cast of fine quality that made the searching worthwhile. Here again, the better samples seem to come from the exposed washes in the hillsides and roadways. Quartz of different colors and sizes is more prevalent, though not as desirable as the limb cast.

The fossil plants displayed at the Dubois Museum came from the Tee-pee formation of this area. Finding that formation would be a rewarding experience that will require some exploration and persistence. In the search keep your eyes peeled for other treasures along the path.

APPENDIX A: *PUBLIC LAND AGENCIES*

Bureau of Land Management

Wyoming State Office
2515 Warren Avenue
P.O. Box 1828
Cheyenne, WY 82003-1828
(307) 775-6256

Casper District Office
1701 East "E" Street
Casper, WY 82601-2167
(307) 261-7600

Worland District Office
101 South 23rd
P.O. Box 119
Worland, WY 82401
(307) 347-9871

Rawlins District Office
1300 N. Third Street
P.O. Box 670
Rawlins, WY 82301
(307) 324-7171

Rock Springs District Office
Highway 191 North
P.O. Box 1869
Rock Springs, WY 82902-1869
(307) 382-5350

National Forest

National Forest Service
Regional Office
11177 West 8th Avenue
Denver, CO 80215
(303) 236-9427

Bighorn National Forest
1969 South Sheridan Avenue
Sheridan, WY 82801
(307) 674-2600

Medicine Bow National Forest
2468 Jackson Street
Laramie, WY 82070-6535
(307) 745-8971

Shoshone National Forest
225 West Yellowstone Avenue
Box 2140
Cody, WY 82414
(307) 527-6241

Black Hills Natonial Forest
Ranger Station
P.O. Box 680
Sundance, WY 82729
(307) 283-1361

Wyoming Highway Department of Transportation

Cody Branch
2530 Beacon Hill Road
Cody, WY 83036
(307) 587-2220

Necastle Branch
600 South Seneca Avenue
Newcastle, WY 82701
(307) 746-3551

Thermopolis Branch
538 North U.S. Highway 20
Thermopolis, WY 82443
(307) 864-3200

Wind River Indian Reservation

Shoshone and Arapahoe Tribes
1 Washakie
Fort Washakie, WY 82514
(307) 332-3040

Fossil Butte National Monument
Box 592
Kemmerer, WY 83101
(307) 877-4455

Yellowstone National Park
P.O. Box 168
Yellowstone Nat. Park,
WY 82190
(307) 344-7381

APPENDIX B: *ROCK SHOPS*

Bill's Rock Shop
1720 East Monroe
Riverton, WY 82501
(307) 856-3857

Bohemian Metals
118 West 16th Street
Cheyenne, WY 82001
(307) 778-8782

Canyon Rock Shop
331 Yellowstone Ave.
Cody, WY 82414
(307) 587-9524

Castro's Rock Shop
Box 36
Encampment, WY 23825

Coulter's Rock Shop
1503 11th
Wheatland, WY 83875
(307) 322-9432

Crystal Clear
130 West 2nd
Casper, WY 82604
(307) 235-4906
C U Rock Shop
Corner of California and 2nd
Shoshoni, WY 82649
(307) 876-2579

Don's Rock and Gift Shop
8917 Hwy 16 West
Buffalo, WY 82384
(307) 684-7983
Open May 1st to Nov. 1st.

Earth Light Stone Fantasy
430 South Wolcott
Casper, WY 82604
(307) 472-7426

Eloxite Corp.
806 10th Street
Wheatland, WY 82201
(307) 322-3050

Green Gold
215 South 1st
Laramie, WY 82070
(307) 742-0003

House of Wyoming Jade and Art
136 South Wolcott
Casper, WY 82604
(307) 234-0867

Norman's Rock Shop
240 N. 8th Street
Lander, WY 82520
(307) 332-2441

Rick's Rocks
108 1/2 South 7th
East Riverton, WY 82501
(307) 856-3506

Rose's Rocks and Gifts
5026 W. Lafayette
Casper, WY 82604
(307) 234-0767

Severn's Studio and Fossil Quarry
500 Loma Vista
Kemmerer, WY 83101
1-800-281-9402

Torrington Rock Shop
Route 1 Box 491
Torrington, WY 82240
(307) 532-5938

Shell Gem and Rock Shop
Box 136, Shell Route
Greybul, WY 82426
(307) 765-2841

Tynsky's Rock Shop
706 Dewar Dr.
Rock Springs, WY 83655
(307) 362-5031

APPENDIX C: *ROCK CLUBS*

Casper Gem and Mineral Club
P.O. Box 1182
Casper, WY 82602-1182

Cheyenne Mineral and Gem Society
P.O. Box 5044
Cheyenne, WY 82003-5044

Castle Rock Gem and Mineral Club
63 Uinta
Green River, WY 82935

Laramie Rockologists
Box 204
Laramie, WY 82070

Shoshone Rock Club
P.O. Box 256
Shoshoni, WY 82435

Riverton Mineral and Gem Society
709 West Jackson
Riverton, WY 82501

Rock Springs Gem and Mineral Club
114 Bellview
Rock Springs, WY 82902-0241

Thermopolis Pick and Trowel Club
P.O. Box 1324
Thermopolis, WY 82443

Index

Rockhounding

R ockhounding Wyoming is an introduction to a
fascinating treasure hunt for those seeking jade, agate
bloodstone, fossils, petrified wood, flourite, or other precio
stones. Although the rockhounding treasures are many in this
vast and sparsley populated state, author Kenneth Graham
points out that "sometimes the joy is in the search itself."
The 75 sites described in this guide will take you across the
red desert to the high mountain majesty of the Big Horns
and Wind Rivers as well as the geologic wonders of
Yellowstone National Park.

Graham, a former hardrock miner, developed an interest
in rocks at an early age. In *Rockhounding Wyoming,* Graham
shares his enthusiasm for rockhounding and his appreciation
for the diverse Wyoming landscape that holds the treasure.
Each description provides detailed information complete with
maps on how to find the remote as well as popular digs, what
will likely be found there, the tools to bring, the best season
to visit, the appropriate vehicle to drive, or when to lace up
your hiking boots to get to those out-of-the-way places.

Be sure to take along *Rockhounding Wyoming* to plan
your next rockhounding adventure.

ISBN 1-56044-445-2

51295

FALCON

9 781560 444459

♻ Text pages printed on recycled paper